HAUNTED AKRON

JERI HOLLAND

CONTRIBUTING EDITOR KEN SUMMERS

Haunted America

Published by Haunted America
A Division of The History Press
Charleston, SC 29403
www.historypress.net

Illustrations by John Holland.

First published 2011

Manufactured in the United States

ISBN 978.1.60949.367.7

Library of Congress Cataloging-in-Publication Data
Holland, Jeri.
Haunted Akron / Jeri Holland, with contributing editor, Ken Summers.
p. cm.
Includes bibliographical references.
ISBN 978-1-60949-367-7
1. Ghosts--Ohio--Akron. 2. Haunted places--Ohio--Akron. I. Summers, Ken,
1979- II. Title.
BF1472.U6H636 2011
133.109771'36--dc23
2011027329

Notice: The information in this book is true and complete to the best of our knowledge. It is offered without guarantee on the part of the author or The History Press. The author and The History Press disclaim all liability in connection with the use of this book.

*This book is dedicated to my uncle, David E. Holland (1945–2011).
He provided me with ideas, historical facts, support and "pronunciation
corrections" throughout the research period of this book. He was not a fan of
the paranormal per se, but we shared a great interest in American history. Rest
in peace. I love you Uncle Dave.*

CONTENTS

PREFACE

I think I've always been aware that ghosts exist, but never consciously did I experience an actual apparition until I was seventeen.

My grandfather had passed away the previous winter, so I made an effort to help out whenever I could. My grandmother lived in a beautiful house that my grandpa had built in Stow, with a large yard in front and in back. It was wonderful, but it could be an awful lot of maintenance. One day, when my grandmother went out of town, I picked up my brother, and we headed over to her house to do some yard work. Together we mowed the yards and trimmed the weeds before heading inside for a drink and a break. My brother headed for the upstairs restroom while I went for the basement bathroom.

I spotted a box of my grandfather's things downstairs and started rummaging through them. I called to my brother to come look. As we started reminiscing over his various hobbies—like dressing up in costumes (Santa Claus, a clown and so on) for people living in nursing homes—we heard the heavy front door open. Then, after about five seconds, it closed with the loud bang of the knocker hitting against the wood. I looked up, expecting someone to call out our names, but there was no sound except for heavy footsteps walking over to the top of the basement stairs.

We walked over and looked up the stairs, giving each other really puzzled looks. I grabbed hold of my brother's shirt in both excitement and fear. In my head, I knew that grandpa had built this house well; there was no way it could creak or knock without someone walking around upstairs. Without a doubt, I had heard that front door open and close and then someone walk to the top of the stairs. Just then, we heard whoever (or whatever) it was walk away from the stairs and down the hallway, into my grandfather's old bedroom. Then the bedroom door shut. My brother, having heard every noise I had heard, grabbed my old childhood baseball bat from the corner of the basement and headed up the stairs. I, of course, stayed downstairs where it was safe. I could hear my brother walk from the top of the stairs down the hallway into my grandfather's bedroom. I didn't hear him open grandpa's door, but I did hear him looking around and going into my grandmother's room. He went through the rest of the house before coming back downstairs to tell me that there was no one in the house except us. He had looked under beds, in closets—everywhere. He saw no one.

But there was something strange about my grandfather's room. Not long ago, my grandmother turned it into a TV room. There wasn't even a door on his old room anymore. I looked my brother in the eyes and said, "Grandpa?" His eyes grew slightly larger, and he nodded once before we headed upstairs together.

I had experienced my grandfather's ghost before this day. Months before, when my grandmother was sick, I stayed overnight in my grandfather's room several times (before it was turned into a TV room). Each night, I heard his rough hands slide against the wooden door as he slowly opened it to go to bed. It took a few times before I realized who it was. Originally I thought it had been my grandma wanting me to keep my door open, but when I would get up to check on her, she was always sleeping soundly in bed. I gradually came to the conclusion that it was actually my grandpa.

We gathered up our lawn tools and put them away in the garage. We had enough excitement for one day and decided that it was time to leave. As I was backing my car down the driveway, I glanced behind me to make sure that I was still on the drive. As I turned forward, there he was—my grandfather stood at the picture window in the living room, watching us leave. I reached over to smack my brother's arm or leg to get him to look at what I was seeing. Within seconds, he was gone. Vanished. But I knew—and my brother knew—that we had just seen my grandfather seven months after he passed away from a brain aneurism.

ACKNOWLEDGEMENTS

K en Summers, this book would never have been finished even remotely on time without you. I thank you for assisting me in research and editing all of my late-night dribbles the last few months. I can't wait to collaborate with you on our upcoming project.

I would like to thank my mom for reading to me and taking me to the library when I was young; it instilled in me the importance of the written word. Come to think of it, you're still taking me to the library and reading to me.

Alan, Jill and Joe, many thanks for allowing me to hang my towel with yours.

To my best friends and my CVP posse—Gayle, Alan and Don—I have so much fun exploring historical sites and haunts with you. I love you guys and I'm looking forward to many more years.

My family and friends (including several "madams"), I love you and thank you all so much for your support and encouragement, especially during the last few months.

And last but certainly not least, much appreciation goes out to every single person who donated his or her time, photos and information that went into writing this book. The Summit County Historical Society, the Northampton Historical Society and the Akron–Summit County Public Library Special Collections were exceedingly important as well.

Introduction

The August 26, 1837 edition of the *American Balance* gives the dry details of Akron:

The village of Akron is situated in the South West part of the County of Portage, in the State of Ohio, 33 miles from Cleveland, on the Ohio Canal, at the Portage Summit, and at the point where the Pennsylvania and Ohio Canal unites with the Ohio Canal. The village extends along the Canal from Lock 1 at the South end of the Summit, to Lock 15, being nearly one mile. Akron was laid out in the Spring of 1825, very soon after the Ohio Canal was laid out, was then covered with timber; but the forest was soon removed and the village rose rapidly, for a short time. The place proving unhealthy during the several succeeding years was, in a measure, abandoned till 1830. A new impulse was then given to the place by reason of a large water power being accumulated at that point.

Before the Ohio and Erie Canal was constructed between 1827 and 1832, Akron was an inhospitable swamp. Disease wiped out many settlers, and after five years of struggle, the place was abandoned. It wasn't until these waters were drained away by workers that the land became useful for building and farming. Since that time in 1830, Akron exploded in population, construction and wealth. The canal made Akron what it is. It brought the mills and factories that made the city famous. Brand names like General Mills, Quaker Oats and so many others started out in this city.

City of Akron postcard. *Courtesy of the author.*

What began as a simple canal town became an industrial giant. Men like Harvey Firestone and Frank Seiberling turned Akron into the "Rubber City"; at one time, it was home to all four major automobile tire companies: Goodyear Tire and Rubber, Firestone Tire and Rubber, BF Goodrich Corporation and General Tire. Blimps soared over the city. Millionaires were made through technological advancement.

But every town has a dark side. Since the first white men and women arrived at this high ground, Akron has been synonymous with death. Early pioneers faced attacks by Native Americans. During the rough early canal days, brawls, knife fights and murders were common in tough neighborhoods and taverns. Crime was everywhere. Dangerous working conditions at factories cost the lives of many more Akronites through the twentieth century. There were bootleggers and gangsters throughout its history. There were riots and mayhem. Akron's past is steeped in blood.

It should be no surprise, then, that the city is full of strange tales and ghostly encounters. There is a never-ending list of tragic tales, grisly homicides and sad stories from inside the city limits and beyond. Yet there are other haunting stories of love and attachment. Not all of Akron is blackness and misery. Some of the spooky stories of the Rubber City are based in happiness.

Main Street. *Courtesy of Cuyahoga Falls Library.*

With that said, what follows is a veritable smorgasbord of Akron ghost stories, from historical haunts to a firsthand ghost-hunting account, along with haunted locations that anyone can currently visit. I've even included fascinating articles from the 1800s telling of certain people and places being haunted. There are murders, train accidents, suicides, drownings and natural deaths. The stories include witches, Indians, robbers and axe-wielding murderers—all truly documented.

I thought that writing about history would be easy. I found out otherwise. In writing about history, you try your best to share the facts without prejudice but without ever completely accomplishing it. When I or anyone writes a history-referenced story, you press on your readers an opinion. I have noticed while reading and researching all these years that each local historian who wrote articles or books shared a personal viewpoint. For example, there are those who agreed with the white settlers taking over Native American lands, while others sympathized with the Indians. Some authors even attempted to state facts regarding the paranormal, but you can always tell if they were believers, skeptics or downright cynics. I thought about these opinions and biases as I wrote each chapter. I wanted to portray the facts, yet I didn't want to lead the reader toward any form of prejudice. I'm not certain I entirely succeeded.

Be that as it may, I wrote this book with all of the historians' stories in mind, along with today's reports and experiences. I did the best I could at combining historical facts with storytelling. Even as a paranormal investigator, I had no idea before writing this that there were (and still are) so many ghost stories to be told from Greater Akron. I hope I have been able to give you a glimpse into the city's haunted history and present.

THE STONE-THROWING GHOST

S tone-throwing poltergeists have been around since at least AD 500, when Helpidius, the personal physician of Theodoric the Great (ruler of the Ostrogothic kingdom in modern-day Italy), was inundated with falling stones. For a number of months, his home in Rome became famous for the "flying stones," which dropped down on his roof from invisible sources. Again in AD 858, a farmer along the Rhine River near Bingen, Germany, found himself attacked by falling stones. He believed that a demon was assaulting him, and a priest was sent from Mainz to rid his body of the aggressive spirit. As the priest began the exorcism, a flood of stones struck him from behind.

On November 29, 1591, the Lee family was bombarded by stones inside their home in Oxfordshire, England. The rocks varied in size from small pebbles to small boulders weighing upward of twenty-two pounds. They scoured the place for clues; there was no perpetrator to be found and, more surprisingly, no holes in the ceiling where the stones materialized. These falling rocks stopped in May 1592 when their eldest son, twenty-two-year-old George, died. Across the Atlantic ocean, another stone-throwing poltergeist began an attack on the home of George Walton in Portsmouth, New Hampshire, in June 1685. A shower of several hundred pebbles fell on the roof of the house. The family rushed outside and found themselves in the middle of a rain of stones. They could see that the pebbles were appearing out of thin air several feet above the house. The shower soon stopped, but it repeated a few days later and continued randomly several times until around November, when the attacks ended.

Then, on an autumn day in 1878, it happened in Akron, Ohio. German-born Michael Metzler and his wife, Maria, had immigrated to the United States in hopes of a better life. They lived for some ten years in Akron until 1878, when Michael and his family moved into a larger brick house situated at 1219 High Street. The area was known by locals as Hell's Half Acre—a blue-collar neighborhood with a reputation for brawls caused by drunken Akron Iron Company workers. Michael and Maria lived in this rough neighborhood with their six children, ages one through thirteen, as well as Maria's seventy-two-year-old mother, Bridget Noss. Michael supported his large family by working as a plasterer at a local factory.

On the bright Tuesday morning of October 8, Maria Metzler was husking corn in their adjacent field when she began being pelted with stones. Unable to find the source of her attack, she ran for the cover of her home. A short while later, her children were outside carrying out their chores when they, too, were struck with rocks varying from a walnut to a chicken egg in size. Finding shelter inside their home, they discussed the incidents and came to the conclusion that someone was playing a nasty prank.

At dusk the following evening, Mrs. Metzler again attempted to husk corn in the field. To her surprise, it happened again. More stones, this time accompanied by clumps of earth, flew at Maria. The outdoor events continued, and by Thursday morning, the stone hurling invaded the safe haven of their home. Maria and her ten-year-old daughter Emma were standing outside by a door that led to the cellar when a large pebble was hurled from inside, striking the young girl in the face. The oldest daughter, Mary, was sitting in a chair inside the home when a stone struck her. At times, pieces of coal and brick were thrown in place of the stones. All of these objects appeared to fall straight out of the ceiling or were launched mysteriously from the dark corners of the room.

News spread quickly throughout the town's 16,500 residents. Friends and neighbors gathered to keep vigil at the house, watching for poltergeist activity. Reactions were similar to what you might expect in today's modern times. Some people laughed at the Metzler family; others wanted to get a piece of the action. A few people had theories on how and why it was happening. Rumors spread rapidly, from mundane trickery to supernatural forces. Perhaps Bridget Noss was a witch. Surely one of the Metzler daughters had become quite crafty at throwing things discreetly.

Several journalists visited the Metzlers' home throughout their ordeal and became part of the story when they, too, were showered with wet, warm rocks. It wasn't long before the story became nationwide news—a

Above, left: Maria Noss Metzler. *Courtesy of Joe Metzler.*

Above, right: Michael Metzler Jr. *Courtesy of Joe Metzler.*

difficult feat to accomplish 130 years ago. "So great has the excitement become that on Sunday, it was estimated that nearly two thousand persons visited the premises," reported the *Akron City Times* on October 16. "In the evening, the crowd took the form of a mob, and there were numerous altercations and disturbances."

By the following week, the distraught family had had enough; they called in professionals for help. Mr. Metzler summoned Reverend John Baptist Broun, pastor of St. Bernard Catholic Church, to conduct an exorcism of the rock-throwing entity. Reverend Broun arrived at the Metzler house at 10:00 p.m. that evening and prayed for the departure of the evil presence. As soon as he finished giving the holy rites, two stones fell at his feet, barely missing him.

In the 1929 *Akron Topics* magazine, reporter William Montgomery Clemens (nephew to Samuel Langhorne Clemens, better known as author and satirist Mark Twain) recalled his own visit with the Metzlers and what he dubbed the "Stone-Throwing Ghost" in 1878:

We entered the living room and closed and locked the two windows and doors. Now I sat next to the grandmother and held both of her hands. The little girl was perched upon the lap of my companion. Mr. Metzler was away at the factory where he was employed. Mrs. Metzler sat near the stove, knife in hand paring potatoes. At her feet was a large pan. Thus we had set the stage for tragedy or for comedy.

And what happened? I was asking Mrs. Metzler for her possible explanation of the manifestation. There were tears in her eyes as, holding the knife in an outstretched hand to emphasize her words, she cried, "It is a curse upon this family."

At that moment a small stone the shape and size of a hickory nut, fell, apparently from the ceiling, and struck Mrs. Metzler on the arm. The stone was warm and wet. Later a larger stone—the size of an egg—fell and struck me on the shoulder—a slight touch like a tap of a finger; the stone fell at my feet, but did not roll or move from where it fell. Like a piece of putty it clung to the floor.

Still other stones fell on that eventful morning all coming, apparently, from the ceiling. We watched for their coming too, and all appeared to have their origin eight or ten inches below the unbroken ceiling plaster. The stones did no damage but they caused deep wonderment.

Two weeks later, it all ended just as mysteriously as it had begun. The events at the Metzler house were never explained. To this day, the incident remains an unsolved mystery. The farm was razed many years ago. A parking lot now occupies the land where the home once stood, on the east side of what is now South Broadway Street, about three hundred feet north of East Voris Street in South Akron.

Were Bridget Noss, the suspected witch, and her granddaughter Emma in cahoots on a masterful prank? Or was something far more sinister behind the Akron poltergeist activity and other cases throughout history?

THE JUVENILE DETENTION HOME MURDER

"Mrs. Bonham?" called Ruth, a seventeen-year-old inmate at Summit County Juvenile Detention Home, to the motherly matron.

"Yes, dear," Eula Bonham answered through the locked door of the second-floor girls' dormitory room.

"Will you fetch my scarf that I left in the common room?" Ruth asked with a nervous giggle.

Thinking that her girls were becoming quite forgetful lately, the gray-haired matron agreed to the request. "Certainly."

At 8:30 p.m. on that November evening in 1955, two of the girls huddled in the dorm trying not to show how scared and nervous they were; they stooped behind their three roommates, who hid on either side of the door. One girl was given instructions to cover the matron's mouth. Two other girls held the belts to be used to bind her arms and legs. A fourth girl readied herself to hold the old woman down while the last teen would shove a washcloth, soaked in ammonia she had hidden in a cold cream jar, into her mouth.

These five teenagers, aged fifteen to seventeen years, all had a past that had landed them inside the Summit County facility. Zelda was the sixteen-year-old wife of a fugitive who had escaped from a prison in West Virginia. She had been arrested the previous November; authorities had hoped that she would provide information on his whereabouts. Shirley and Margaret, both fifteen, were placed in the detention home after running away from home several times. Fifteen-year-old Merl had been involved in a robbery at knifepoint. Ruth had been relocated to Akron from the Girls Industrial

School in Lancaster, Ohio, in order to testify at the trial of a man accused of contributing to her delinquency.

Eula Bonham had been a matron at the Summit County Juvenile Detention Home, built in 1930 on Power Street, for sixteen years. In her years of service, she developed a positive reputation and was well liked by both her fellow employees and the teenage girls in her care. On this particular day, Sunday, November 27, Eula was particularly happy, as giddy as a schoolgirl. Her first marriage had ended in divorce, yet on December 1, Mrs. Bonham had plans to remarry, this time to a wonderful man. Though she was exhausted and ready for bed, Eula was willing to go out of her way to help out her girls. Little did she know that this simple act of fetching a scarf would put an end to her happiness, her plans to marry and her life.

When Mrs. Bonham returned with the scarf and unlocked the door, the five girls sprang into action. Merl, fifteen, later recalled the event for the press. "I was supposed to hold her mouth so she couldn't scream," she said. "But I couldn't because she had cold cream on, and her skin was slippery. Then, four of us knocked her down on a bed, and I tied her hands and feet." (Bruising on Bonham's throat indicated that she'd been strangled at some point.) "Before we left, I hit her twice over the head with a shoe because she was still struggling. Then, I dropped the shoe and ran."

The other girls in the dormitory said that Merl and her accomplices had been rehearsing the escape for some time; they had discreetly stocked up on ammonia in an empty cold cream jar. In order to keep the others quiet, the gang of girls threatened to kill them if they spoke a single word about their plot to anyone.

The five girls ran out into the hallway, past the other locked dormitory rooms, and down into the basement. They used a shovel to smash out a window. The boys' dormitory supervisor, twenty-nine-year-old Ralph Roebuck, heard the commotion from the first floor. He was watching a group of twenty-nine boys in the recreation room. Later, he reported that he witnessed the five girls escape out the smashed window, but he made the decision not to chase them for fear that the boys would try to escape, too.

One by one, they crawled out to experience that wonderful feeling of freedom. Unfortunately for the girls, this freedom was confusing and frigid due to a few major oversights. Late November in Ohio can be quite cold, yet none of the girls thought of grabbing a coat. They also didn't plan where to go once they escaped the building or even how they were going to get there. While they were standing in the freezing cold, deciding where to run, the

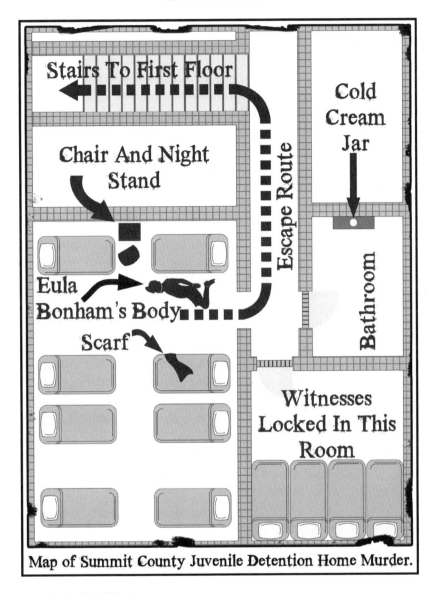

Map of Summit County Juvenile Detention Home Murder.

Illustration by John Holland.

matron lay unconscious inside the dorm, quietly choking on the cloth. She died of suffocation within fifteen minutes of her attack.

Just a few hours after the escape, Merl and Margaret walked into the police department and turned themselves in. Zelda surrendered to police after hiding in cellars for nearly twenty-four hours in below-freezing temperatures near the detention home. Ruth and Shirley, however, hitched a ride with a truck driver at a service station up to Cleveland. The duo ended up riding back with the driver and were dropped off the following day at another gas station in Akron. They hid there to keep warm. The station attendant alerted the authorities, who found them huddling in the corner of the restroom. Ruth, covered in crime cult tattoos, said that she was sorry but added, "We wouldn't have got caught if we'd moved fast."

Following their surrenders and captures, the other girls also expressed their remorse for Eula Bonham's death. They said that the ammonia cloth was meant to knock her out, not kill her, while they escaped. They pled guilty to manslaughter, and each received sentences of up to twenty years. Two of the girls were sent to Marysville Reformatory. The remaining three served their time at a girls' industrial school in Delaware, Ohio.

On December 1, instead of a beautiful wedding, mourners gathered at Akron Baptist Temple for a gloomy (but love-filled) funeral. Eula Bonham was laid to rest in Glendale Cemetery.

In 1960, the Summit County Juvenile Detention Home was moved to a new facility on Dan Street. The Power Street building was then used for a while by the Summit County Children Services Board before it was turned into a women's prison from 1982 to 1990. Today it serves as a residential correctional facility for Oriana House, a chemical dependency treatment agency.

In the many years following her murder, some Akronites believe that Eula Bonham's ghost has haunted the Power Street facility where she passed away. They believe that the second floor, which housed the girls' dorms where she was killed, has the most ghostly activity. The room where Eula died has a particularly uncomfortable vibe to it.

In the late 1980s, when the women's prison was at that location, inmates and employees claimed to hear footsteps, moving furniture and other peculiar noises within the building. Windows opened and closed on their own accord throughout the second floor, and televisions and radios turned on and off at random times. Even the front desk typewriter sporadically would type as if operated by unseen hands. One witness, a female deputy, claimed that a pen flew out of her pocket and that a pizza slice levitated out of her hand. Her cigarette, sitting in a nearby ashtray, was knocked to the floor.

Last names have been omitted for reasons of privacy.

THE GHOST BLIMP

One of the most intriguing mysteries of World War II—and one still not solved—is the disappearance of Flight 101 and its crew. It's a different sort of story, and not your traditional type of haunting, but the tale involves an Akron resident and a Goodyear airship designed and built just outside of Akron, Ohio.

At 6:03 a.m. on the morning of August 16, 1942, Flight 101 departed Treasure Island, California. Navy Airship L-8 was one of twelve blimps that composed Squadron 32, which routinely patrolled the Pacific Ocean, carefully watching for Japanese submarines approaching the coast. On board was twenty-seven-year-old Lieutenant Ernest D. Cody and Ensign Charles Adams of Lakehurst, New Jersey, who set a course west out over the vast ocean. Cody, the pilot of the blimp, had lived in Akron before arriving at Moffett Field and was married to Helen Haddock, the daughter of Akron Goodyear employee Richard L. Haddock and his wife, Juanita.

The mission was a relatively simple one: conduct an antisubmarine patrol along the coast of California, traveling from Treasure Island (just north of the Golden Gate Bridge) to the Farallones, a chain of small islands some thirty miles west, before heading north to Point Reyes and returning the blimp to Moffett Field at the southern end of San Francisco Bay. Normally, the flight called for a crew of three men, but foggy weather conditions on the bay reduced the crew to two in order to make up for excess water weight from condensation. At 7:42 a.m., Lieutenant Cody radioed the base to inform staff that he and Adams had located a possible oil slick on the ocean.

On the morning of August 16, 1942, the L-8 departed Treasure Island, California, for a routine antisubmarine patrol. On board were Lieutenant Ernest Cody and Ensign Charles Adams, who set a course west out over the vast Pacific. *Courtesy of the U.S. Navy.*

The men were heading to its location for further investigation. That was the last message ever heard from the two men aboard the L-8. In fact, it was the last sign of Cody and Adams ever recorded.

Three hours passed without any word from the blimp. Nervous commanders prepared to dispatch a rescue crew to search for the airship. As the blimp floated over Mussel Rock, onlookers could see that the blimp was in trouble. Bruce McIntyre, one of the first eyewitnesses to see the aircraft, shared his observation with a reporter: "It was dished on top and appeared to be drifting with its motors off...It was so low I could see shroud lines [used by the ground crew for landing and takeoff] almost touching the hilltop."

Thirty minutes later, the gray airship was spotted resting against a cliff along the Pacific coast eight miles south of San Francisco. Civilians nearby at Lake Merced Golf Course witnessed the L-8 soaring inward from the sea and watched as the blimp disappeared behind two hills, where it snagged on a cliff near Fort Funston Park. The gondola carved deep scratches into the cliff as it smashed against the shore, bending the propeller blades and packing the right engine with dirt and debris. As a rescue crew approached, the blimp gently rose and began to drift inland. As it flew toward Olympic

Golf Club, one of the two depth charges (antisubmarine explosives) on board the airship was dislodged from its rack and fell to the golf course near the ocean. The shore patrol immediately notified Moffett Field.

The L-8 had begun to deflate, losing altitude as it headed straight for Daly City. The plummeting airship brushed the rooftops of houses and smashed into telephone lines, sending a shower of sparks over the neighborhood. A utility pole on Bellevue Avenue finally caught the blimp with enough force to bring it down at an intersection in the center of the 400 block. It struck two automobiles and touched down on one wheel, making a near perfect landing and lurching to a stop.

The airship lay still where it fell. There was no movement other than the crowds of people rushing toward the balloon. William Morris, the first person to reach the scene of the accident, quickly checked the inside the gondola. Mr. Morris, a volunteer firefighter, stated that "the doors were open and nobody was in the cabin." The crowd gasped in horror. Lieutenant Ernest Cody and Ensign Charles Adams were nowhere to be found.

The partially deflated navy airship L-8 drifts over Dale City, California, on August 16, 1942, with no one aboard. The airship had left earlier that morning on a routine patrol with two men aboard; they were never seen again. *Courtesy of the U.S. Navy.*

The L-8 came to rest in the center of the 400 block of Bellevue Avenue in Daly City, just two blocks south of the San Francisco–San Mateo County line. *Courtesy of the U.S. Navy.*

Firefighters, called to the scene from a training exercise burning brush in the nearby hills, arrived just as the blimp touched down. They sliced through the blimp's envelope, hoping to find the crew trapped inside, but there was no sign of the two navy men. What made it even stranger was that there were no outward signs of stress or turmoil. The throttles were at idle, there was fuel in the tanks and the cabin door was open. A check of the helium gas valves showed that they were set precisely as they should have been. Even the radio was still in good working order. All in all, the airship was perfectly airworthy.

Navy salvagers arrived at the scene within an hour to take command of the wreckage. They found all the parachutes accounted for and stowed in their compartments, as was the life raft for emergency use. Two life belts, required to be worn by the crew at all times, were missing and assumed to be on the bodies of Cody and Adams at the time of their disappearance. Lieutenant Cody's hat sat where he had placed it on the instrument panel.

A locked briefcase containing a confidential file with classified information was still inside the gondola.

Immediately, the navy launched an extensive search of the Pacific coastline for Lieutenant Cody and Ensign Adams. Lieutenant Commander Donald M. Mackey of Moffett Field released an official statement: "The Navy is positive it has covered all the ground area covered by the blimp. It is positive the men were NOT in the ship at any time it traveled over land." A weeklong search of the Pacific Ocean by the Coast Guard continued. Navy patrols near the Farallon Islands were placed on high alert in hopes that the men might still be found. Not one trace ever surfaced.

Cody's Akron relatives couldn't understand how such a tragedy had occurred. "My son-in-law was a levelheaded and unexcitable sort of person," Juanita Haddock told a reporter in 1942. "He would have used his head in any emergency, I believe." The U.S. Navy conducted a thorough investigation. The last radio message from Flight 101 had occurred at 7:42 a.m. There was no response from the airship at 8:50 a.m. when the blimp was contacted by Treasure Island. Therefore, whatever happened to the two naval pilots occurred between these times.

The Naval Board of Inquiry heard testimony from the crews of two commercial fishing boats in the area of the oil slick reported by Flight 101 at the time of its radio message. They, too, saw the oil slick and observed the L-8 descend to three hundred feet and circle the dark patch of ocean. The crew quickly brought up their nets and motored away from the area, expecting the blimp to drop its depth charges in case a Japanese sub had run aground. Instead, the blimp quickly lifted off without dropping any explosives and disappeared into the clouds. The sudden liftoff could be explained by the loss of the crew, suddenly sending the lightened craft skyward, but at no time did either crew observe anything—or anyone—drop from the airship.

Blimp L-8 quickly acquired the nickname "the Ghost Ship." Tales of the mysterious disappearances of Cody and Adams were embellished by the public. Wild rumors began to include false details about half-eaten sandwiches and still-warm cups of coffee being found in the gondola. Even to this day, a variety of theories circulate to explain the strange tale of Flight 101. Some speculate that the men were captured by the Japanese or had plotted to desert the military. A few people even suggest that the men were abducted from the blimp by aliens, yet none of these claims is supported by any existing evidence.

A full year later, the two missing navy men were officially declared dead.

*Above:*This gondola, designated C-64, was refurbished after the war and was eventually returned to service as one of Goodyear's public relations airships, the *America*, based in Houston, Texas. *Courtesy of Goodyear.*

Left: The *America* was retired in 1982. In 2003, the gondola was donated to the National Naval Aviation Museum in Pensacola, Florida, and has been restored for display. *Courtesy of Goodyear.*

Following the crash landing, the navy once again took possession of the airship. The envelope was severely destroyed during and after the accident, but the gondola was still in sound shape. It was repaired and used by the navy for training purposes. When its wartime service came to an end in 1945, it returned home to Akron. Flight 101's metal gondola was stored by the Goodyear Tire and Rubber Company at Wingfoot Lake Hangar until 1968, when it was rebuilt for use on the Goodyear blimp *America*. Based in Texas, the *America* flew over televised sporting events across the United States from 1969 until 1982, when it was retired. The gondola once again was placed in storage at Wingfoot Lake until 2003, when Goodyear donated the gondola to the National Naval Aviation Museum in Pensacola, Florida. The museum restored the gondola to its original World War II appearance for display in the exhibit halls. The black "L-8" lettering has been returned to its ghostly gray sides.

There's an old adage from the navy that its men never abandon their ship. Could the two men still be with the gondola?

BOTZUM

A REAL GHOST TOWN

Dozens of long-forgotten towns are scattered across northeastern Ohio. The canal era and railroad boom were responsible for most of these "ghost towns." When the canal closed, railroads moved on and other cities grew, these bustling crossroads were abandoned. While some still exist as a scattering of houses, others have returned to the earth, leaving a few stone foundations in the woods.

One such town, called Botzum, developed while the Ohio and Erie Canal was under construction in the late 1820s. It was located at the intersection of Bath and Riverview Roads, six miles north of downtown Akron in the former township of Northampton (now a part of Cuyahoga Falls). Originally called Yellow Creek Basin, the town eventually included a hotel, a general store, a tavern, a post office, a school, a train station, a cemetery, a covered bridge, a blacksmith shop, a sawmill, a gristmill, a boatyard, two warehouses and a dozen homes. At its height, the population reached forty residents.

A warehouse and store were first built by Nathaniel Hardy in 1825 near where Yellow Creek meets the Cuyahoga River. Hardy had helped build the canal before settling the area, and he erected a hotel and tavern for canal laborers and travelers. The town, which soon became known as Niles, had a tough reputation. Brawls often erupted when canal workers got drunk at the tavern, and horse thieves and counterfeiters lurked in the woods.

Nicholas Botzum and Thomas Owen ran rival mercantile establishments, each occupying opposite sides of the canal. On the spillway for waste water from the canal north of town, two sawmills were built to manufacture

The remains of the John Botzum General Store. *Photo by Jeri Holland, 2011.*

All that remains of the Botzum Hotel in 2011. *Photo by Jeri Holland.*

Above: The John Botzum General Store in 1875. *Courtesy of Dreama Powell of the Northampton Historical Society.*

Below: My seven-year-old nephew examining the Botzum Store ruins. *Photo by Jeri Holland, 2011.*

lumber for use in Cleveland. A post office was established in 1866, and the Valley Railway established a station there in 1880. The post office and station were called Buckeye until 1893, when the town's name was changed to Botzum.

John Botzum, the namesake, was one of the early settlers of the region. Originally from Germany, Botzum had moved his wife and nine children to the United States in 1836, where their last child, Conrad, was born that same year. They settled in Niles in the late 1830s; his family prospered and gradually purchased the majority of the land in the area.

In 1922, the Botzum family sold eight hundred acres to Akron for construction of a sewage treatment plant. Upon completion of the facility, the city tore down the laborers' shacks, along with several of the nearby abandoned town

The Botzum Covered Bridge was destroyed after an overloaded truck attempted to cross. *Courtesy of the Cuyahoga Falls Library.*

buildings. The one-hundred-year-old covered bridge was destroyed ten years later after an overloaded truck attempted to cross. The remaining buildings were torn down or left to decay. Some worn boards, a few foundations and weathered cornerstones and steps are all that is left of the town, scattered among the flowers and hedges of ghostly homestead gardens. The Conrad Botzum Farmstead, now restored by a nonprofit organization, is one of the last standing reminders of the village.

The villagers who didn't move away remain buried at the town burial ground. Botzum (or Yellow Creek) Cemetery stands on a hill west of the village along Yellow Creek Road. This pioneer cemetery contains about 175 graves (some accounts list 300 burials); fewer than a dozen headstones now mark the location. The oldest stone remembered, according the Northampton Historical Society, is that of an eighty-four-year-old woman who died in 1779. Most of the burials took place in 1836, a particularly brutal winter that cost the lives of many of the town's children. Over

My nine-year-old niece paying a visit to the Botzums at the Yellow Creek (Botzum) Cemetery in 2011. *Photo by Jeri Holland.*

the last hundred years, many of the sandstone and marble markers were knocked over by grazing cows, damaged by vandals or destroyed by the Ohio weather. The graves of the Botzum family, along with many other influential villagers, stand forgotten. Among those missing tombstones is a murder victim, forgotten by time but still seeking answers.

The Murder of John Tedrow

Botzum was the scene of a fatal tragedy in 1882. In the rough-and-tumble canal town, the quiet autumn serenity was shattered when a tale of murder (and grave robbing) was born.

John Tedrow was a pleasant and well-liked young man in his late twenties who had lived in the fertile valley north of Akron for several years, working as a farmhand at whatever homesteads he could find employment. He was tall with dark mulatto skin and muscular from years of hard labor. A good worker who knew the value of a job well done, Tedrow's work ethic earned him a good reputation as a hired hand. This all changed, however, every time he reached for a bottle of alcohol—one of his favorite leisure activities. When intoxicated, Tedrow was very unstable and ready for a fight.

On the night of Friday, October 27, the hotel beside the Cuyahoga River in Botzum was the scene of a benefit dance hosted by the Buckeye Band, a music group headquartered in a first-floor room at the hotel and composed of young men from Botzum and neighboring villages. The event attracted a local crowd of about forty teenagers and young adults to the second-floor ballroom. Among the many guests was Thomas Brook, a twenty-four-year-old from England, who was courting Ellen Thomas, the twenty-two-year-old daughter of the hotel's middle-aged owner, Seth M. Thomas.

Earlier that afternoon, Tedrow, along with one of his white friends, had spent some time in Akron. By the time the two men caught the evening train back to town, Tedrow was a bit tipsy. The two companions ate supper at the hotel before heading over to the nearby saloon, where they continued to drink heavily. When they returned to the front steps of the hotel, the dance was well underway, and a few guests lingered on the porch. In a fit of drunken rage, Tedrow grabbed hold of Seth Thomas and started pushing him around, knocking him off the porch. Tedrow then turned his attention to Thomas Brook. He jumped at Thomas and somehow managed to tear the boy's suit jacket.

Staggering into the upstairs ballroom, John Tedrow reportedly unleashed a flood of foul language and threatened the young crowd. Most of the attendees ignored his outburst and didn't allow the ranting to ruin their fun evening. After saying his piece, Tedrow and several of his friends left for the saloon once again.

John Tedrow was murdered with an axe on October 27, 1882, in Botzum, Ohio. *Courtesy of Dreama Powell of the Northampton Historical Society.*

Meanwhile, Thomas Brook went into the kitchen and sent Seth's son, sixteen-year-old Charles Thomas, up to the ballroom to fetch his sister, Ellen Thomas, and her friend, Mabel Gray, to come down and repair his badly torn jacket. After sewing up the damage, Thomas, Ellen, Charles and Mabel decided to head back to the dance. As they passed into the hall shortly before midnight, they heard noises coming from the room used for rehearsals by the Buckeye Band. Brook thought that Tedrow must have come back. He rushed through the washroom and headed toward the band room in case Mr. Thomas needed any help fending off Tedrow. Before he had even reached the band room door, Seth Thomas burst through it and rushed past, pursued by a drunken, enraged Tedrow.

When Tedrow came face to face with Brook, he seized the Englishman by his collar and began to yank and push him around. Ellen hurried over to the commotion and pinned herself between her boyfriend and Tedrow. She put her hands on Tedrow's cheeks, looked anxiously into his eyes and said, "Tedrow what do you mean? Do you know where you are?" As Ellen stood holding his face, an axe fell and struck Tedrow on the side of the head, dropping him instantly to the ground. He was dead by the time his body hit the floor.

The incident brought the dance to an abrupt end. Thomas Lancaster accompanied Thomas Brook on a wagon ride to Akron. There on Market Street, close to 3:00 a.m., they found a police officer named David K. Bunn. Brook placed himself in the custody of Officer Bunn and, at Brook's request, was taken to the home of respected lawyer and Civil War veteran General Alvin C. Voris on Fir Street. After a brief discussion of the events in Botzum, General Voris sent Thomas Brook to Akron Jail.

How did the axe appear in the washroom of the hotel? And who put it there? It seemed so conveniently on hand at that particular moment. These burning questions were answered at trial.

The axe that delivered Tedrow's fatal blow to the head belonged to Charles Thomas, Seth's son, and was left as usual at the woodpile behind the hotel on the night of the murder. Some testimony showed that Seth had handed the axe to Thomas Brook when he rushed into the washroom. In another scenario, Seth hurried to the woodpile, where he grabbed the axe, returning to the washroom the moment that his daughter stepped between her lover and Tedrow. He handed the axe to Brook, who raised the weapon and fatally struck Tedrow.

These revelations led prosecuting attorney Charles Baird to charge both Thomas Brook and Seth Thomas with murder. Marshal William H. Ragg arrested Seth and sent him to jail, awaiting the preliminary hearing held on November 4 before Mayor Samuel A. Lane. The preliminary trial lasted two days; after thorough examination and interviews of the many witnesses present that night, charges were dropped against Seth. It appeared that Thomas Brook was solely responsible for the crime. When his decision was announced, Mayor Lane addressed the court:

> *The history of this case is largely a repetition of the great majority of the homicides of the world, in that it is directly the result of the excessive use of intoxicating liquors, the evidence developing the fact that not only was the victim—naturally as amiable as men in general—rendered quarrelsome thereby, but that several, if not all, the actors and witnesses of the fearful tragedy (except the ladies) were more or less under their baleful influence.*

Thomas Brook stood before the Court of Common Pleas facing a second-degree murder charge in January 1883. The grand jury listened to prosecuting attorney Baird's meticulous examination of the evidence and indicted Brook, who entered a plea of not guilty. For the trial, Governor Sidney Edgerton was assigned to aid the prosecution. For Brook's defense, General Voris was joined by fellow attorney Jacob A. Kohler.

The three-day trial opened with a revelation from none other than Brook's sweetheart, Ellen Thomas. When testifying, Ellen admitted to asking her boyfriend why he did it in the moments after Tedrow was struck down dead. "It could not be helped," he answered, adding, "Don't cry for me." Ellen initially refused to answer when asked by the prosecution if Brook told her he expected to be hanged for Tedrow's death. Only after Baird threatened Ellen with jail for contempt of court did she scream, "Yes! He did!" It also was her testimony that she didn't witness who had delivered the axe blow, since she was still holding Tedrow's face at that very moment and her back was to the assailant.

After a short deliberation, the jury returned with a verdict. Instead of second-degree murder, Brook was found guilty of manslaughter. General Voris filed a motion for a new trial, claiming that alcohol and the defenselessness from its consumption were the real causes of the crime. It was overruled by Judge Tibbals. Brook was sentenced to twelve years at Ohio Penitentiary in Columbus. Beginning on March 31, 1883, Thomas Brook served about three years in prison—the same length of time he had lived in America—before being paroled for good behavior and moving to the Cleveland area for the remainder of his crime-free life.

This was not the end of the story, however. Before Brook even stepped into a courtroom, there was more trouble for Tedrow in Botzum. His body was laid to rest in Botzum Cemetery on October 29. The following day, a bizarre story was found in the *Akron Beacon Journal*:

> Among the baggage…checked at the Valley depot in this city this morning was a trunk…accompanied by a fine-appearing, well dressed gentleman. There was nothing strange in this…but the fact that blood, human blood, was seen to flow pretty freely from the trunk whenever it was turned over, and [seeing] that the man who was with it watched it so carefully and objected to its being ended up as is common, caused the baggage men at the station named to [become] suspicious that that trunk contained more than ordinary goods.

Rumor of a crime quickly spread. When word reached an *Akron Beacon Journal* representative, he set out to unravel the mystery. Through a coworker, he was told about the murder of a black man named Tedrow in Botzum a few days before the strange cargo appeared on the Valley Railway. After some investigation, the reporter became convinced that the body in the train trunk was that of John Tedrow, despite the fact that officials in Botzum claimed that Tedrow had been buried the previous day. And his hunch proved correct. Without widespread knowledge, a Cleveland medical professor had been given proper permission to send a doctor and an assistant to the town of Botzum and claim the body for a cadaver. Tedrow's body was exhumed without much affair on the evening of October 29 and then was loaded onto a train bound for Cleveland the next morning. The body had not been drained beforehand, which caused the blood to leak out through the trunk (and spill the suspicious "crime" rumor along the journey north).

The Botzum Depot, which operated from 1880 until 1929. *Courtesy of Dreama Powell of Northampton Historical Society.*

From that day forward, body claimants have been required to use properly sealed containers for cadaver transport.

Turmoil and unrest are believed to be two of the reasons why ghosts appear. The tale of John Tedrow is a classic example. If anyone hasn't been able to rest in peace properly, it would be John Tedrow—and possibly even Thomas Brook, who may have lived the rest of his life filled with guilt. Today, if you sit among the trees in the northeast corner of the intersection of Riverview and Bath Roads, where the infamous hotel once stood, you still can hear someone running. Is it Brook forever running from the scene of his crime? Or is it someone, like one of the Thomas boys, running to get the axe? On other still nights, the silence is broken by a man's scream. Perhaps it is Tedrow's final moment of agony or the echo of his last drunken, brawling night of life.

Recordings of electronic voice phenomena (EVP) have captured what appears to be the voice of John Tedrow. Often he will greet you cheerfully as you sit down and ask questions. Sometimes you can even get him to tug on your jacket. If you're lucky (or unfortunate) enough, you might catch a glimpse of Tedrow, wandering the woods in search of the man responsible for his premature death. He appears just as he looked that fateful night: a six-foot, dark-skinned muscular man with a swollen right eye and a bloody forehead, with blood dripping from the right nostril. If you see him, fight the urge to run; just tell him who's responsible.

BOTZUM MOUND

Nearly twelve thousand years ago, humans began living in the Cuyahoga Valley north of Akron, but they left very few traces of who they were. These early people faded from sight into the mists of ancient times without leaving a written history. Then, about 2,500 years ago came a new breed of large-statured people. Aptly named, the Mound Builders were the first native people in the United States to build mounds made of earth, sometimes mixed with stone. These mounds were used for fortifications, burials and ceremonial use. The Mound Builders have been classified into three different cultural groups: the Adena (1000 BC to AD 200), the Hopewell (AD 300 to 700) and the Mississippian (AD 700 to 1500).

Today, the Akron area is rich with remnants of Hopewellian society—like in the forgotten ghost town of Botzum. On the southwest corner of the old village is a "star mound," so named for its shape, spanning over one hundred feet across and thirty feet in height, making it one of the largest such mounds in the area. It was excavated years ago by archaeology students from the University of Akron, but nothing was discovered inside. They did, however, prove that it was an unnatural (or man-made) earth formation. About four hundred yards away, a smaller mound can be found closer to Riverview Road.

Also located within the immediate area is a Native American burial ground. In 1843, this burial ground was first disturbed when the canal was widened. The Valley Railway cut through the center of the burying ground in 1880, unintentionally excavating forty skeletons. The corpses were only two feet below the surface and lying in irregular rows without any sort of uniform style. Some were buried with their heads pointing east, while others faced to the west. There were males and females and children, the latter accounting for about one-third of the burials. The soil surrounding each buried body was black.

The smaller Botzum earth mound built by the Mound Builders long before the latter Native Americans arrived in the area. *Photo by Rodney Johnson.*

One evening late in April 2002, Dave Holland (my cousin, friend and fellow ghost hunter) and I decided to hike to the smaller of these Indian mounds for a preliminary ghost hunt. We were armed with digital and analogue recorders. As we walked down the Towpath Trail, with only the moonlight to guide our way through the dark, the woods felt eerie yet very calm. About a quarter of a mile down the trail, we approached the small earthen mound, which appeared out of place on the flat surrounding land. We weaved our way through the brush and started climbing up the ten-foot mound. It was covered from top to base with trees of varying ages.

Dave and I settled in, prepared to spend at least thirty to sixty minutes recording in the hopes of capturing an EVP. We could hear the sounds of coyotes far off in the distance—one of my favorite sounds of the night. For about ten minutes we sat atop the mound, asking questions like, "Is there anyone here that would like to speak with us?" and, "Can you tell us your name(s) please?"

Without even realizing it, the sounds of the coyotes grew incredibly loud. We couldn't even hear ourselves speaking to each other. Without a doubt, they had surrounded the Indian mound. Howling came from every direction. While the educated side of me knew that coyotes do not hurt people or chase humans, I was still overcome by immense fear. *Why would they surround us like this? Why are they howling for so long without stopping?* Dave and I looked at each other and, without saying a word to each other, collectively ran down the south side of the mound and through the woods until we reached the path. As soon as we reached a point where I could see the car in the parking lot, we both stopped dead in our tracks and looked at each other. I silently sent a mental *What the heck?* over to my cousin. It had all stopped. No howling, no coyotes…just silence.

"Where did they go?" Dave asked.

"I'm not sure," I responded. "I didn't even see them while we were running down the mound."

Remembering the recorders (that we had thoughtfully remembered to pick up) in our hands, we hit play on one to see if we were just crazy or really had heard what we thought we had heard.

Sure enough, the recording captured the howling of the coyotes getting closer and closer until you couldn't even hear our voices. As the playback continued, we were in for an even bigger surprise. In the midst of the coyote cries, we heard a woman's bloodcurdling scream! Chills ran down our spines. It was just too real. And thinking that it might have been real, we decided to look around the area and see if anyone was hurt. We even checked the nearby roads to see if someone's car had broken down. We never saw anything out of place that night, but the haunting scream certainly stuck with us. Even now, when I hear a nearby coyote howl, all I can think of is that strange night on the Indian mound.

Remember, it is illegal to desecrate or excavate federal lands for the discovery of Native American remains and objects. If you are asked by park officials to leave or remove yourself from regions containing Indian artifacts, please do so. We need to help protect our historical areas for our future generations to see.

LIBERTINE DIXON

THE "BRAVE" INDIAN HUNTER

The Dixon family lived in the pioneer wilderness near Steubenville, Ohio, in the latter half of the 1700s. They were accustomed to all kinds of hardships; with nine children, they were poor and struggled to make a living off the land as best they could. Even though the father, Thomas Dixon, was a weaver by trade, he never seemed to make ends meet. The children slept on the cabin's dirt floor, in the loft or in the straw-filled barn. The Dixons made do with what they had, which was very little. The rough life created a tough family unafraid of taking risks; long before the widespread westward movement by settlers into the Ohio lands, they relocated to the deep forest of what is now Green Township, near the intersection of South Arlington and Boettler Roads. The Dixons were rumored to be the very first white family to settle in the area.

One of Thomas's sons, a rough-looking young man named Libertine (sometimes referred to as "Liberton" in historical texts), made fast friends with the area's Native Americans, and he spent the majority of his time living with them in and around the East Akron area. But the peaceful coexistence didn't last forever. One particular evening, seven years after the family had settled in the Ohio frontier, there was a confrontation between Libertine and a native man around a campfire. The Indian became enraged at the white man and lunged at him with a knife. Libertine fled from the camp, followed closely by the native, but stumbled and fell over a brush pile. The brave leaped right on top of him, dropping his knife. Libertine sprang into action, seizing the weapon and killing the Indian.

Libertine knew that after committing such a crime against a native he could never return to the tribe, so he decided to return to the haunts of civilization. The Indians discovered the body of their slain brother, and the tribe gave chase to Libertine on his way back to the white settlement. Libertine hid behind a tree when they started firing at him, but the trunk was so small that he was hit seven times. Still, he managed to escape and afterward settled back in Green Township, where he eventually married Hannah Pelton Culver and fathered four children. From that day forward, though, he became a bitter enemy of the Indians. According to Libertine Dixon's own accounts, many Indians died by his hands in the coming years after this first incident.

Forever the loner type, Libertine spent most of his time in the woods with his only constant companion: a long, black, ungainly looking rifle that he always spoke of with respect. In fact, he spoke of his rifle as it if were a living person, calling it by the peculiar name of "Starling." Many people, including

Illustration by John Holland.

44

Libertine himself, spoke of the wild stories of complete disregard for life on the part of Libertine, or rather that of Starling. The gun became his alter ego and a convenient excuse for his bloodthirsty habits. He walked around both the forest and town with Starling proudly perched on his shoulder. Thinking that any Indian who had a chance to kill him would immediately do so, he always took the opportunity to shoot first.

One such "opportunity" involved the tragic death of Wampetek, the chief of a tribe of about forty Indians living near Turkey Foot Lake. These mild-mannered, unoffending American Indians had never harmed any white settlers. Libertine often quarreled with the chief about a bee tree, of which they both claimed ownership. Shortly after one such quarrel, Wampetek went missing. The sound of a rifle shot came from the nearby woods, followed some time later by Libertine Dixon emerging from the trees. A local asked Libertine what he had shot.

"I shot at a deer," he replied.

"Where is your prize?"

Without much emotion, he answered, "I missed the animal."

Dixon was a crack shot with Starling and never missed an object he fired at. No one in the area believed his story. What sounded more believable was that he had shot Chief Wampetek—not a deer—because the chief was never seen again. It was assumed that the chief was fatally shot from behind near Indian Pond and that Libertine then threw the body into the pond. A few days after the chief went missing, some men found the remnants of a fire near the pond that contained the half-consumed belongings formerly owned by Wampetek.

When Libertine was hunting the following spring, he strolled to the edge of the same pond, where he discovered an Indian fishing from a birch-bark canoe. As he hid behind a tree, "Old Starling thought he would speak to the fellow." The native fisherman was so frightened by the shot (which pierced his side) that he let out a horrific scream and fell into the lake, never reappearing. The smoke had hardly cleared when another Indian, who had been building a fire nearby, rushed to see what his companion had shot. As the Indian combed the lake for his friend, Dixon slipped away and quietly disappeared.

These and other tragic incidents have given rise to stories that the area is haunted by spirits of the natives. Indian Pond still exists to this day, albeit not nearly as clean and picturesque, about one mile west of Arlington Road where Turkeyfoot Lake Road meets Cottage Grove. On bright, moonlit nights, you can hear the unearthly yell from the Indian in his canoe still to this day. If you listen closely, they say that at times you can even hear the residual sounds of Libertine throwing Wampetek into the water. Throughout the 1800s, residents of the town of East Liberty would travel miles out of their way, taking the long route to avoid the pond rather than pass the still waters of Indian Pond, to avoid seeing the shadowy form of the Indian gliding over the placid, misty surface of the lake in his birch-bark canoe or hearing the agonizing final scream as his ghost fell into the water.

On another occasion in the early years of the nineteenth century, a handful of Indians entered the town of Middlebury (now East Akron) and stopped in at the grocery store, where Libertine Dixon was doing some shopping. As they entered the front door, a terrified Libertine hurried out the back door and sprinted to his cabin. He told his family that the Indians were after him and that if anyone needed him they should look for him in the woods. Libertine then grabbed Starling, some bullets and gunpowder and a healthy supply of dried beef before disappearing into the wilderness. In a weeks' time, he returned to tell the story for himself:

I went into the woods and kept low until they left, then I followed them, but [I] kept myself so concealed that they did not suspect me. They were, however, on the lookout for someone, and scoured the woods, until finally they seemed to give it up, and started toward Old Portage. One, however, watched the ravine closely where the Big Cuyahoga flows through the chasm near the Big Falls, and once, as he was hanging by one arm…to a hemlock tree on the edge of the rock, and looking closely up and down the valley, I stepped out from [my hiding place] behind a big chestnut and "Starling" spoke to him. But "Old Starling" spoke so suddenly that it scared the fellow, and he jumped off the bank on to the rocks below some forty feet and killed himself. After a while, I went up to him and as he didn't seem to want his gun and other things any longer, I took them.

Of the dozens of stories passed down regarding Libertine's Indian hunting and "bravery," it is believed that most of them could have been embellished. The stories told by Libertine himself even may have been totally fiction. There is good reason to suspect that, by reading his accounts of incidents and his Starling, Dixon may have suffered from some sort of mental disorder, but if these stories of Indian attacks are falsified accounts by an unbalanced man, why would he spend his later years—long after the natives had left the area—in fear of Indians? Though Libertine was allegedly not afraid of any living thing, his later years were consumed by a fear of the dark. For the final half of his life, he refused to set foot outside after dark. Libertine Dixon, the "brave hunter" and self-proclaimed Indian combatant, was utterly afraid of the ghosts of the Indians whom he had killed.

Long after moving farther west, he fully believed (as told by area settlers of the time) that the dead natives were still hunting for him and would never give him peace until he took his last breath. Their ghost lights were said to glow throughout the woods of Green Township. The lights terrified him and circled around him whenever Libertine went out to his barn or was doing his evening chores. The lights frightened him so much that he would tend to his chores early and head for the safety of his house well before dusk.

Libertine Dixon finally found his peace of mind in 1830 when he passed away. Or did he? Some say that he's still walking the woods of Green with Starling at his shoulder, looking for one final "opportunity."

WILL-O'-THE-WISPS

In ancient folklore, our ancestors gave many names to the strange lights that would sometimes appear at dusk or during the night over swampy areas and marshes. Katharine Briggs's *A Dictionary of Fairies* contains a broad list of names for the same phenomenon, though the place where they were witnessed (graveyard, swamps and so on) significantly influenced the naming. A light that came from the home of a dying person and wandered into the cemetery was called a corpse candle. In the woods and glens, they called them fairy fire. Occasionally, the phenomenon was classified by the spectator as a ghost, fairy or elemental. In today's terms, it might be referred to as an "orb" by paranormal enthusiasts, but it was the resemblance to a flickering lamp and tendency to recede if approached that gave these lights their most common name in the 1800s. First in Britain and then America, the townspeople called such lights jack-o'-the-lanterns, or will-o'-the-wisps.

While many of us are familiar with the Irish tale behind the jack-o'-lantern—of Stingy Jack, who cheated the devil and was doomed to roam the earth carrying a lantern made from a hollowed-out turnip—few of us have heard about the origin of the will-o'-the-wisp (or will-o-wisp, as it is also known). This tale was just as bizarre. It was said that St. Peter had hired a blacksmith named Will to give his horse a new shoe. Will, an old man not long from the grave, was granted one wish by the saint; he asked to be made young again. Will then spent his perpetual youth living a rowdy life of debauchery, luring travelers to their deaths with the eerie glow of his wisp (or burning bundle of straw). This story gave the phenomenon its Latin name: *ignis fatuus* or "foolish fire."

In the early settlement of Green Township, part of modern metropolitan Akron, the low grounds were well known for sightings of the will-o-wisp. Settlers believed these "spook lights" to be the spirits of Indians who had returned to visit their old hunting grounds. Long before the War of 1812, the Native American population in Ohio was great. However, the Indians sided with the British during the war, so those remaining were forced by the settlers to leave the area. When the town pioneers first appeared in the region in about 1809, the remains of old Indian forts and wigwams could still be seen.

The main Indian territory here had been located close to the headwaters of Nimishilla (or Nimisila) Creek, north of Greensburg Road. The local area was known for its many streams and lowlands. The name of the creek came from the language of the original inhabitants of the region. "Nimishilla" was the Indian name for a shrub called black alder by the first European settlers. The plant—now known as common winterberry—grows in wet areas and along stream banks.

A favorite hunting ground for the Indians was east of the creek, just north of Akron-Canton Airport today. This site appears to have been selected by the Indians because it was lightly wooded, with very little undergrowth, and was elevated above the surrounding lowlands. Many arrowheads, hatchets, skinning knives and other tools have been unearthed there. A large quantity of flint chips was found here as well, although it is not known where the Indians found the stone. This site appears to have been where they carefully carved their stone hatchets and knapped and shaped the arrows to prepare for their hunts.

Found throughout this particular spot of elevated land were rocks that varied in size from a baseball to a human head. These were arranged in piles, averaging four feet by ten feet in length and width. Traditional native stories mention such stone heaps, called cairns, which held the cremated ashes of warriors and chiefs. Many cairns have been built over the past five thousand years throughout the northeastern United States by Native Americans, not only for burials but also for ceremonial purposes. These particular stone mounds contained no bones or other human remains, so they likely marked a site used for ceremonies.

Native American ceremonial sites such as these, much like modern outdoor churches or shrines, were places where Indians came to pray and practice their religion. Documents, diaries and letters belonging to early

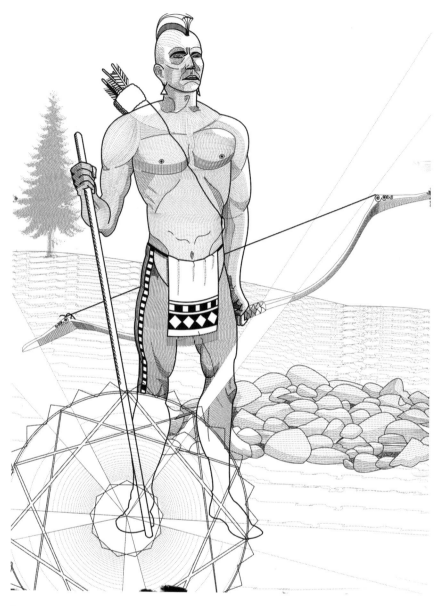

Green Township had rock mounds, will-o-wisps and the Ottawa tribe. *Illustration by John Holland.*

Christian missionaries and travelers mention that when passing these cairns, their Indian guides would stop and solemnly add a stone as a religious observance. Most—if not all—cairns have been removed and destroyed by modern construction, but many survived for decades after the natives were driven west. If the cairns were not in the way of fields or buildings, most early farmers left them untouched out of curiosity or respect—or possibly even superstition.

One early settler in Green Township attempted to desecrate one of these cairns. According to the historical writings of General Lucius V. Bierce, after the man had dug three or four feet into it and almost reached the bottom, he was "seized with a supernatural fear, and abandoned the enterprise." No matter how well armed the early settlers were, many were far more terrified of Indian ghosts than of the living natives. The faintest glimpse of a harmless will-o-wisp would cause a strong man to tremble as he made his way through the dark forest. His imagination would turn the orb of light into the spirit of the "red man."

This Halloween, if you find yourself carving a pumpkin, take a moment to think back to the stories of Stingy Jack and Will. Remember that our modern candlelit jack-o-lanterns are based on age-old stories of spook lights and will-o-wisps. And if you find yourself near Green, be careful as you walk through the woods between Nimisila Reservoir and Greensburg, for the natives may have returned to their ancestral hunting grounds to rebuke the white settlers for their deception and lies.

Should you come across any of these remaining cairns in your exploration of northeastern Ohio, please remember that Native Americans still consider these places sacred to their spiritual beliefs. Please be respectful when exploring cairn sites by not digging for, removing or adding stones or artifacts. Instead, take photographs and leave everything as you found it.

THE OHIO AND ERIE CANAL

A kron had two main canals during the nineteenth century. The Pennsylvania and Ohio (P&O) Canal, opened in 1840, was the area's east–west waterway and brought machines, supplies and people to the growing city. The outgoing boats exported wood, wheat and wool from factories. More historically important, the Ohio and Erie Canal fueled Akron's growth when it was opened in 1827. It didn't take long for new technology to replace the historic canal. After the rise of railroads in the mid- to late 1800s, the slower waterways could not compete. The P&O Canal only ran for forty years before closing down. Canals started being used for fishing, ice skating and swimming. Other portions of the canal were totally abandoned; citizens used the section through Main Street as a dumping ground for trash and debris. Then, during the Great Flood of 1913, the locks of the Ohio and Erie were dynamited by city workers to relieve the rising floodwaters threatening downtown Akron. A surge of water crashed through the remaining locks both north and south, destroying the canal beyond repair. Today, many segments of the canal are part of national parks and trails throughout northeast Ohio.

Before the opening of the canal systems, thousands of men were hired to dig the canal "ditches." They labored away during daylight hours, earning only thirty cents, a bowl of stew and a shot of whiskey each day and using only the tools available at the time: picks, shovels, plows and wheelbarrows. It was backbreaking labor for the men, many of whom were Irish immigrants. Digging went slowly through mosquito-infested swamps in hot and muggy summer weather. Hundreds (if not thousands) of workers were bitten and ended up with malaria, working through the high fevers and chills. Back in those days, they referred to it as "canal fever." Disease was easily spread in the tough working conditions on the canal, and many workers died during the canal's construction. The workers were buried along the canal in unmarked graves, usually not far from where they fell dead. The men claimed that "for every mile of the canal, an Irishman is buried" (at 308 miles long, that's a lot of bodies); it was often referred to as the "Irish Graveyard." There were many other deaths, as well, not only while building the canal but both during and after its operation, too. Suicides, murders and drownings happened frequently. Sounds like a hotbed for paranormal activity, right?

Over the years, we have used "bait" (or what Everyday Paranormal dubs as "era cues") to gather information on the hauntings of a particular area. Using objects, sounds and actions familiar to people from a specific time frame aids in finding out what ghosts and spirits are in an area and why they remain. Bait is based on the theory that you can prompt paranormal activity from ghosts of a specific decade by presenting them with stimuli from their time period. In this case, while investigating along the canal or lock, you might begin by playing songs sung by the families who lived on canalboats ("The Jolly Boatman" or "Take a Trip on the Canal"). Other such bait might include calling out familiar orders to the ditch diggers or the lock tender, or even dressing in 1830s period clothing.

By using such methods, we have found that many of the Akron locks along the canal appear to be quite haunted. We have found, using audio recorders and multiple K2 electromagnetic frequency (EMF) meters, who we think are haunting the old Akron canals. The following locks are some of my personal favorites.

LOCK 4: WAS IT MURDER OR SUICIDE?

On April 22, 1886, the headline of the *Summit County Beacon* blared, "THE BODY OF ED. F. MOORE FOUND IN THE OHIO CANAL WITH MARKS OF VIOLENCE PLAINLY VISIBLE." On Thursday, April 16, a man named Rankin O. Sprague was walking along the towpath one afternoon when he spotted a peculiar object in the water near Lock 4. At first he thought it was a stone. But after taking a better look, he realized it was the corpse of a man. Sprague hollered to several men nearby, and within a few minutes they dragged the shockingly gruesome sight onto the canal shore. The dead man's old, worn clothes, as well as his face and hands, were coated with a heavy layer of mud. When they washed the mud from the face, the water revealed the white features of the very red and bloated body. One man checked the pants pockets to try to identify the deceased. Numerous papers and receipts were found, one of which was a receipt for $207.60, signed by M. Swinehart, for saloon fixtures from a bar located on the corner of North High and Furnace Streets. The name on the receipt was E.F. Moore. Other bills and receipts were made out to the same name, so they concluded that the man was none other than Edward F. Moore.

Very little was known about Ed Moore. He had moved to Akron on November 9, 1885, where he rented a small room at the Pfeiffer House Hotel on West Market Street. Moore kept to himself and always dined alone. The majority of his time was spent at the saloon drinking and spending his money on loose women. Moore tried to start a saloon fixtures business, but drinking and brotheling took a higher priority, it seemed. By mid-February of the following year, Ed was destitute; he had sold his saloon fixtures to liquor wholesaler Mr. James Bruot for half the sum he paid for them. From that day on, Moore became a beggar and survived only by the grace of others. Whenever he could get away with it, Moore began sleeping in the gasworks and paper mill. Three weeks before his body was found, Ed had lost all hope and routinely talked of suicide. He wrote a letter to Albert Spiller, an old acquaintance, informing him that, in case he was found dead, he wished his body to be returned to his hometown of Minerva for burial. This letter was later used as part evidence of a premeditated suicide. Ed Moore's body was found near Lock 4 about fifty feet from his favorite haunt—a popular Akron house of ill repute.

Undertaker George Billow was notified, and the body of Edward Moore was taken to the morgue for examination. Moore's face showed evidence of a violent end. On his forehead was a bruise made by a blunt instrument; the throat showed signs of strangulation. Billows speculated that the body had been left in the water for nearly a week. But within a few days of inspecting Mr. Moore's corpse, considering the letter and public threats against his own life, Billows announced that the death was an apparent suicide. However, word began to spread throughout Akron that before his death Moore had been involved in arguments with several local men.

What do you think? Murder or suicide? History records the death of Edward Moore as a suicide, but words beyond the grave tell a different story. EVP captured near the lock suggest it was murder.

LOCK 10: ACCIDENTALLY DROWNED

William Welton, the owner of a grocery store adjacent to Lock 14, was walking along the towpath of the canal just after 4:00 p.m. on November 1, 1887. When he reached Lock 10, he saw the body of a man floating in the water. Calling for assistance, Welton and the men who came to his aid fished the man from the Ohio and Erie Canal. His body was still warm, but not breathing. Had they known how to perform CPR back in those days, the man might have survived; but, alas, the poor man passed away. A crowd of onlookers soon gathered at the lock to see the latest victim of the canal. Sadly, no one was able to identify the old gray-haired gentleman.

Summit County coroner Albert H. Sargent arrived on the scene and, after an investigation, found that the body belonged to that of Laughlin Douds of Avon Springs, New York. He was visiting his family in Cuyahoga Falls and Akron for a few months at the time of the accident. The seventy-eight-year-old man was said to have been very intelligent and well read, much loved by his family, yet he was a feeble man suffering from partial paralysis. This was by no means a handicap, for Douds spent a large amount of his time walking around the city, soaking in the sights and sounds of Akron.

After the crowds dispersed, and Douds's body was placed with his family, two men visited the coroner. They had witnessed the old man walking alone along the canal and also saw him plunge into the lock. Since that day, Laughlin Douds has reappeared at Lock 14—at least in spirit.

This particular drowning victim's ghost is a bit different from your typical haunting. People have encountered Mr. Douds in broad daylight strolling along the towpath, asking where his nephew's home is. It appears that in his old age, the man suffered from memory problems as well as physical disability. When visitors attempt to help him find his way, they discover that he's disappeared into thin air.

LOCK 14: MULTIPLE ACCIDENTS

Little is known about the details surrounding a January 1858 accident at Lock 14. The body of Daniel Quinn was found in the Ohio Canal lock at the site during that frigid month. The Irishman had been missing for four days.

The site of many drownings, Lock 14 is a part of the Ohio and Erie Canal. *Photo by Andrew Borgen.*

Flash forward twenty-seven years later. On a beautiful spring afternoon in April 1881, Akron Iron Company workers George Stone and Joe Oster headed out to the wetlands near the canal to harvest a bushel of watercress. Somewhere between home and the canal, the men took a side trip for liquor, which they started drinking while on their hunt for the leafy greens. According to Oster, the duo became separated late in the day. The last time he saw George Stone that evening, he was completely intoxicated.

When George didn't return home to his mother's house by morning, she became extremely concerned. Her other son, Robert Stone, and family friends Thomas Higgins and Mark Edwards were sent out to find him. At about 10:00 a.m. that morning, they found the thirty-seven-year-old's body floating in the Ohio Canal near Lock 14 under the North Street Bridge. County coroner Almon Brown concluded that George had died by accidental drowning while under the influence of liquor.

Several EVPs have been recorded here. Two of these, from the same evening, are voices saying "accidently" and "drowned." Are they speaking of George or Daniel? Or could one of the men actually have been murdered instead?

LOCK 16: THE GHOST OF CHALKY BROWN

The sound of childlike chatter is one of the greatest sounds on earth, even after death. To most people, the ghost of a child is less threatening and fearful. Such is the case of the haunting at Lock 16. Childlike giggling, talking and scuffling can be heard at this lock. But why, you ask? The reason points to the forgotten tragedy of a life cut all too short.

Back in the 1800s, long before child labor laws, children often started working at a very early age. It was no different for Charles Phillips. In 1883, Charles—nicknamed "Chalky Brown"—went off to work for his grandfather at the age of nine.

On July 18, Chalky Brown and fourteen-year-old George Hoagland were transporting wheelbarrows of fill dirt beside the canal. The two boys were carrying on a fun conversation when, at 9:00 p.m., Chalky accidentally ran into the long wooden handle of the lock gate in the dim twilight and tumbled into the water. The lock only contained six feet of water, but the boy struck his head on the beam across the gate during the fifteen-foot fall. He was knocked unconscious by the time he hit the water.

Seeing that Chalky didn't swim to the top, his friend George jumped into the canal to rescue him but couldn't find any sign of the young boy. Several local men came to the rescue and jumped into the canal water. After a twenty-minute search, the boy's body was found at the bottom of the lock.

LOCK 26: PANCAKE LOCK SUICIDE

On the northern edge of Akron, deep in the Cuyahoga Valley near the Ira Trailhead, is what remains of Lock 26. According to famed canalboat captain Pearl Nye, it was called Pancake Lock because the surrounding land was as flat as a pancake. One hot August evening in 1877, the beautiful, serene area wasn't quite so peaceful. A well-known machinist and veteran named George Pomeroy went there to die. The sad tale all started about two weeks earlier.

Sixty-year-old George W. Pomeroy was a kind husband and a good father. His only downfall was his insatiable appetite for liquor. One evening, George stopped by the bar after work and proceeded to get horribly drunk. He was still highly inebriated and incurable when he drove his wagon home several hours later, so much so that his family fled from their house on Water Street. Mrs. Pomeroy and her children took up residence in another house right across the street. For two weeks, she continued to cook meals for her husband and had them sent over each day. George stopped by several days after the incident to share a noon meal with his wife. They had a pleasant lunch, after which he asked his wife to return home again. Mrs. Pomeroy thought for a moment but politely declined his offer. "I won't come back," she explained to her husband, "until you get yourself some help with that drinking problem of yours." If he showed signs of improvement, though, she promised to come back home.

George left the house numb, but for a short time it appeared that there was hope, even if it were only wishful thinking. He headed over to the canal, and Captain Patrick Killbuck asked him to help lead a canalboat up to Cleveland. George agreed, took control of the horses and started north. The canawlers—as people who made their living off the canal were called—didn't notice anything unusual in George's behavior until 3:00 p.m., when they reached Pancake Lock. After they "locked through" (navigated through the lock), someone saw George leave the horses on the towpath and head over to the nearby fence. Here he lay down, taking out a large jackknife, and quietly sharpened the blade. After testing the edge's sharpness, he raised it to his throat. The steersman, unable to leave his post, saw what George was doing and yelled frantically to anyone who would listen. In one swift stroke, George slit his neck. A man in a nearby field heard the steersman's yell and came running. The cut only broke the skin, so George raised his knife to his neck once again and sliced deeply from ear to ear. This time, he hit the jugular vein. By the time the man from the field arrived at the lock, George Pomeroy was dead.

Today, George still wanders Pancake Lock trying to get people to help him convince his wife to come back to him. He tugs on your shirt and begs for help; if you ignore his pleas, he will stomp right past. But to find him, you have to be patient; his boat only comes through at 3:00 p.m.

HIGH BRIDGE GLENS

More than a century ago, amusement parks were a popular draw to many places in northeast Ohio. Beyond Cleveland's famous Euclid Beach Park, dozens of other parks sprang up from Lake Erie to Springfield Lake in Akron and beyond. These were not the wild amusement parks we know now; early amusement parks were more for fun-filled relaxation instead of thrills and chills. In the late 1800s, the Cuyahoga River north of Akron was the site of one such popular amusement park of the day. Hidden between the steep cliffs of Cuyahoga Falls was High Bridge Glens Amusement Park.

When the park was first opened in 1879, High Bridge Glens advertised a thrilling roller coaster (not what we consider a roller coaster today; this was a round-tracked gravity railway that sent passengers up and down on a smaller loop) and a large dance hall. It also featured a dining hall, a pavilion and a graceful suspension bridge across the Cuyahoga River. Another special section was devoted just to children. Trails along the rocky cliffs led to other picturesque park locations such as Fern Cave and Mirror Lake. People came from as far as Detroit to spend the day socializing, relaxing and dancing by way of the interurban railroads that connected Akron and Cuyahoga Falls to Cleveland.

During the park's heyday, some sixty trainloads and trolley cars of tourists were brought in every day. Towering eighty feet above the Cuyahoga River, the High Bridge (which gave the park its name) provided a grand entrance to the Glens. Travelers stepped down off the trolley at the park entrance on

The Mountain Line prior to the accident. *Courtesy of the Cuyahoga Falls Library.*

the west side near Front Street and onto the steel observation bridge that spanned the river.

The Mountain Line trolley, part of the Akron and Cuyahoga Falls Rapid Transit Company, ran along Furnace Street from Main Street in Akron. From there, it crossed a 325-foot bridge spanning the Little Cuyahoga River and then ran Northwest up a steep incline to Bettes Corners and crossed a 350-foot trestle. The line then followed Home Avenue to Prospect Street, where it went across the High Bridge to Front Street in Cuyahoga Falls. This bridge (now called Prospect Avenue Overlook Bridge) provided a great view of the river and the Glens Park for many years, but it experienced a few tragedies as well.

Gus Shuler and Martha Kline were riding in a horse-drawn carriage to Cuyahoga Falls from Akron on the night of May 9, 1883. Portions of the High Bridge had been removed for repair and a barricade placed at each end to keep travelers from crossing, but it was assumed that the horse knocked down the barricade as it started across. The horse slipped through the hole, somehow finding its footing on a ledge while the carriage carrying the young couple fell to the river below, smashing into shards. Unfortunately, no one noticed the accident until the following morning, when a passerby found the horse still perched on the ledge, waiting to be rescued. A rescue crew searched for bodies in the wreckage, but neither was found. In fact, the search continued for days along the riverbanks without any sign of the couple. It wasn't until two weeks later that Miss Kline's body was discovered. Another year went by before they recovered the only remains ever found of Gus Shuler: his skull.

By the 1900s, High Bridge Glens began to sell liquor. An influx of "young roughs from Cleveland" (as one writer from the *Cuyahoga Falls Reporter* called them) disturbed the serenity of the park. Drunken brawls and violence cut down on the popularity of the Glens. However, the bridge itself also added to the park's demise. On a beautiful Tuesday afternoon, June 11, 1918, the unthinkable happened. The Mountain Line trolley made its usual run around a sharp curve before heading across Glens Bridge toward Front Street. However, it never reached the other side.

The 4:00 p.m. run of the Mountain Line to Cuyahoga Falls was late. Car no. 350, driven by motorman Leroy Bessemer, made a stop on the east side of the Glens Bridge at Prospect Street to let off two passengers and continued onward, crossing the bridge at a slow rate of speed. As the trolley reached the center of the bridge, the front wheels left the tracks. Before Bessemer knew what was happening, the car broke through a section of wooden bridge planks and steel railing, plunging the trolley eighty feet into the Cuyahoga.

A nearby crew for the Akron, Kent and Ravenna trolley on Front Street heard the commotion and ran to help. Other people, both at the amusement park and in town, also heard the crash and rushed to the scene to lend a hand. The AK&R conductor, being small in both stature and build, was tied to a rope and lowered down to the wreck. He later shared his experience with a newspaper reporter:

> *I was the first human being to witness the results of this terrible accident, up close. As I was being lowered down to the wreck, I could only see two bodies…As my main interest was to get aid to the injured, I located the bodies as fast as possible, and had the people on the bridge pull them up. The only person I believed to be alive, and made a determined effort to save, was Luizzi Pellogione, an Italian lad, who had been thrown clear of the wreckage into deep water. His feeble efforts [were] to no avail as he drowned before I could get help to him. By this time, men had reached the scene from other places and I was extremely glad to turn this gruesome job over to them.*

Above: The Mountain Line fell through the Glens Bridge after derailing. *Courtesy of the Cuyahoga Falls Library.*

Left: An Akron, Kent and Ravenna conductor was one of the first on scene. Here he is being lowered on a rope in an attempt to rescue any survivors. *Courtesy of the Cuyahoga Falls Library.*

The car had apparently tumbled end over end as it fell and landed nearly upside down. The roof and sides were crushed flat like a box; in fact, the frame was so devastated by the impact that a small boy could have lifted the remains without any effort. Three holes were cut into the upturned floor of the car to gain entrance to what remained of the inside of the smashed trolley to extract the victims. Fortunately, there were few passengers at that early hour. By some miracle, the motorman, Leroy Bessemer, and a passenger named Henry Van Loosen—both of Cuyahoga Falls—survived.

Strange as it may seem, both Bessemer and Van Loosen, a machinist, were placed in the wagon for dead bodies by mistake. Someone standing near the dead wagon noticed movement and called to a nearby doctor. Upon close examination, the physician discovered that both men were, in fact, still alive (albeit barely). Bessemer had suffered a head wound and a broken leg. Van Loosen had escaped with a skull fracture. After some time, both men recovered fully and lived fairly normal lives into old age. The four dead were identified as Emory Prior, an attorney and secretary of the Falls Savings and Loan Company; C.C. Hoy, a Falls cement block manufacturer; O.D. Gilmore, the trolley conductor; and Luzzi Pellegione, the young Italian Akron resident.

More rescuers arrived to cut holes into the side of the trolley in an attempt to extract bodies. *Courtesy of the Cuyahoga Falls Library.*

From Glens Bridge to the Cuyahoga River is about an eighty-foot fall. *Courtesy of the Cuyahoga Falls Library.*

Those who didn't hear the horrifying crash soon heard the news from their neighbors. It seemed as though everyone in the area rushed down to help or keep an eye on what was happening. The whole town was aghast with horror. Discussion was rampant throughout the huge crowd. The citizens of Cuyahoga Falls could not believe that something like this had happened—again!

The bridge appeared to be quite prone to accidents over the years. Many other stories are relayed to us from local historians. According to Dudley Weaver, a historian from Kent, Ohio, people have fallen, jumped and driven off Glens Bridge since it was first constructed. All of the individuals died from the treacherous fall to the river; however, in December 1969, one man was known to have survived the fall.

Following the Mountain Line accident, the village of Cuyahoga Falls cancelled its contract with the trolley company. The number of tourists dropped drastically, in part from the disaster, but also from the termination of trolley service to the park. Gorge Dam, built downstream by the Northern Ohio Traction and Lighting (NOT&L) Company, had already flooded portions of the park. By 1920, High Bridge Glens Amusement Park was but a memory.

Even today, when the water is low, if you look especially hard you can see the ghostly remnants of the 1918 disaster. The steel frame and wheels of the Mountain Line wreckage below the bridge still rest lodged between the rocks in the river. It was so badly smashed that no attempt was ever made to salvage it. But there might be a few otherworldly pieces of the past as well.

High Bridge Glens is a well-kept secret by the local paranormal groups. Although very active with paranormal activity, it is not a location frequented by many searching for ghosts. During earlier investigations in the Greater Akron area, Cuyahoga Valley Paranormal, the group I founded, has discovered that places once filled with happy entertainment seem more prone to ghostly activity. For this reason, we first decided to test portions of the Glens in 2003. The 120-year-old park seemed to be a prime spot: tragic deaths coupled with millions of hours of pleasure and relaxation. It was a win-win situation on the paranormal front.

We also felt that the rushing river falls would add to the possibility of recording ghost voices on tape. This audio contact with a spirit, known as EVP (electronic voice phenomena), falls under the umbrella term "instrumental transcommunication" (ITC), which refers to any conversations with ghosts, spirits and the dead using electronic equipment including tape recorders, camcorders, telephones, answering machines,

South of the Glens Bridge, within the High Bridge Glens Park area. *Courtesy of the Cuyahoga Falls Library.*

radios, televisions, computers and so on. Messages may or may not be heard while being recorded, but they are certainly heard when you play back the recording.

The Cuyahoga River drops nearly eight hundred feet in a two-mile stretch through Cuyahoga Falls and the Glens, creating rapids and swift rushing water that produce an effect known as "white noise." In electronic recording and communication systems, white noise is a combination of many sound frequencies and sounds a bit like a hiss (or the static from a radio or television not tuned into any station). The efficiency of white noise for EVP recording is debatable by some. Many paranormal researchers insist that it acts as an attractor, immediately drawing in any entities in the area like moths to a flame. We in CVP find that it works amazingly well at High Bridge Glens, though we also keep in mind that other background noise (such as the expressway and other industrial sounds) are present nearby, so the best recording time is very late at night.

EVP captured in this area have included the following: "Get help," "Help me," "Hello," "It's nice to see you" and "Look." Besides the audio evidence at the Glens, investigators have had many personal experiences. A handful of witnesses claim that while visiting the overlook bridge, they either see or feel the Mountain Line trolley traveling toward them across the bridge. While standing on the eastern side of the bridge, people have felt the bridge vibrating rapidly, as if a trolley is approaching. Then, the vibration abruptly stops. Others have seen apparitions of men donning top hats on occasion.

Since 2009, the High Bridge Glens entrance now features a small two-acre park dedicated to the old amusement park. A gazebo, benches and picnic tables are placed throughout the site and are available for public use. A newer, updated bridge leading to a boardwalk brings you close to the raging water and provides a beautiful view. The city's very first state historical marker is located here; it permanently designates the riverfront park and its 130-year history.

During the day, High Bridge Glens is a beautiful place to sit and eat your lunch; it's a peaceful place to sit quietly late at night using ghost-hunting equipment. Anyone under eighteen is not permitted in the riverfront area after 8:00 p.m. unless a parent or guardian is present. Please abide by all laws and regulations and be respectful of the area if you visit.

As an added challenge, we would like you to send any photographs or EVP you capture in this area to hauntedakron@gmail.com. Maybe yours will be posted on www.hauntedakron.info.

THE BLAZING RED BALL

There are people who believe in the paranormal and skeptics who mock the ones who do. It takes an extraordinary experience to change the mind of a disbeliever. In Summit County history, this very thing happened more than a century ago near a small village south of Norton. Two strange incidents occurred one mile south of this town that silenced even the heartiest of critics once seen with their very own eyes.

The townsfolk didn't understand why Johnson's Corners was such a haunted place. It wasn't known for any battles or horrific accidents, nor was it a deserted community full of creepy, abandoned buildings. On the contrary, the farmland was filled with beautiful golden fields of grain. Peaceful country roads were dotted with houses and their well-kept lawns. Yet there was no denying that after dark, unexplainable things happened.

One of the more prominent farmers and landowners in the region was John Breitenstein. His neighbor during the 1880s was an older gentleman by the name of Shaneman who lived in a small house across the road. Shaneman and his wife lived on a prosperous farm, yet they lived frugally and well within their means. It was whispered that the old farmer kept a treasure-trove of money locked away in his small home.

The old man sold a tract of land beside his property to the Carrara Paint Company of Barberton, for which he received another large sum of money. Not long after selling off the land, Mr. Shaneman died suddenly in 1892. Family and friends descended on the house and searched every nook and cranny for the cash. The treasure hunt turned up only $150; no trace of

Shaneman's fortune could be found. The people decided that the money must have been buried or hidden in a secret location. It was so well hidden that no one was ever able to find it.

Beginning on the night following Shaneman's death, an eerie red light began to appear. Mr. Breitenstein later shared his experience in the *Akron Daily Democrat* on August 8, 1902:

> *"Peter Shaffer, John Mong and myself were sitting up with* [Mr. Shaneman's] *corpse. Mong was smoking and Shaffer and I had been talking. All of the sudden Shaffer gave me a nudge and directed my gaze to the ceiling at the corner of the room where the corpse lay, when I saw a sight that fairly made my hair stand on end. What seemed like a ball of fire had started from the corner of the room and was travelling slowly around the ceiling of the room."*
>
> *"Did you see it?" said Shaffer.*
>
> *"Yes," said I.*
>
> *"Let's get out of here," were Shaffer's next words, and we made for home as fast as we could.*

A few nights later, the Shaffer family and other neighbors joined the Breitensteins on their veranda. Without warning, "a bright light as large as a street car lamp" floated up in a field behind the Shaneman house, glided noiselessly down the road past the gathering and headed toward Breitenstein's barn. When it disappeared beyond the barn, everyone broke their silent gazes and ran to the barn in search of the ghost light. But when they arrived at the spot, nothing could be found.

On one occasion, the light appeared at the bedroom window of John Breitenstein and lit the entire room so brightly with its eerie, fiery glow that John awoke, thinking it was daybreak. When John's son, Harry Breitenstein, got married, he moved with his wife into the old Shaneman house. From the moment they moved in, they began to see the light around the house. Harry's family claimed that the bed in one room would shake by unseen forces; all of his family members refused to sleep in it at night. One particular night, Harry ran to his father's house in a panic, screaming that their house was on fire. John and his family rushed behind his house, where they saw a brilliant red light glowing like fire. It lingered for a few moments before slowly dimming into the darkness of the night.

Harry's brother, Milton, was not immune to seeing the ghost light. One evening, Milton came home late and put his horse in the barn as usual. As he stepped into the house, John and his wife saw that he was white as a sheet. "Oh, ma," he whispered. "Come here!" As she peered outside from the door frame, she could see why Milton was so alarmed. There by an old apple tree, thousands of tiny, candle-like lights in every color imaginable danced around the branches. Slowly, they grew and turned into red balls of flame and dropped to the ground, rolling away down the orchard path.

"Folks may laugh if they will, but it is no laughing matter with us who live here and see it," John Breitenstein told the *Akron Daily Democrat*. "What it is I do not know, but what I tell you I have seen, and this is gospel truth."

Rumor quickly spread that the ghost of the old man had returned, trying to show where his money was hidden. There was no telling where or when Shaneman's ghost light would reappear. Sometimes it rose from the fields behind Shaneman's house; at other times it would materialize on the roof. But observations of the red ball of light weren't limited to the Breitenstein family. Nearby residents also began to see the strange ghost light quite frequently. In the summer months, sightings would become less regular, but come each winter the red light would become even more active.

According to Mr. Breitenstein, "Peter Shaffer has told me of seeing the light many times and he isn't a man to lie"; he went on to retell the story as he heard it:

Shaffer, with his wife and two daughters, were passing through the fields back of our house one night, bound for a neighbor's house. The women were walking ahead, when suddenly Shaffer saw the mysterious light moving along beside him. Then one of the girls looked back and with a scream started to run and soon the entire family was running for dear life over the fields. They came to a fence, but stopped not for a moment and how they ever got over the fence not one was ever able to tell. When they reached the road the light disappeared.

Beginning in 1898, Adam Kiehl and his wife lived in the Shaneman house. Mr. Kiehl never encountered any strange phenomena, but his wife claimed to have seen the red ghost light in her room one night. After the Kiehl family moved elsewhere, John Winkleman and his family moved into the old house. No family members ever reported having seen anything supernatural.

At about the same time as the neighborhood struggled to explain the strange lights, another mystery presented itself. This time, the mystery involved something much more unnerving. It all began when Louise and Minnie Shaffer were walking home late one night. The girls noticed a strange "animal" on the road in front of them that came closer and started creeping around under their feet. They tried to kick it away, and when they did it simply disappeared into thin air. A moment later, the shadowy creature was back walking with them. Terrified, the young women ran as fast as they could until they safely made it home.

Peter Shaffer also claimed to have seen the strange animal not long after the girls' encounter. At about four o'clock one afternoon, he went to the Kiehl Coal Mine, just at the rear of Breitenstein's property, to order a load of coal. Beside the chutes, Shaffer saw a figure climbing up the incline. As he drew closer, the figure leaped onto the platform on all four legs. Thinking that it was an employee playing a practical joke, he approached it without hesitation. The thing was not a man but rather some type of gray, semitransparent animal. The beast quickly disappeared into the mine, but Shaffer did not follow it. Instead, he ran for his life until he reached the safety of home.

A few days after Shaffer's sighting, two miners—Jean Cady of Barberton and George Conrad from the small village of Sherman, northeast of Johnson's Corners—encountered a similar gray, phantom animal inside the mine. They rushed toward it, raising their picks and swinging violently, but the beast faded away as they made contact with it. It continued to reappear in other parts of the mine. After several failed attempts to approach it, the men ran home in fright. Cady quit that very day and never entered the mine again. Other men who worked at Kiehl's mine also encountered the strange creature in and around the tunnels. Some were so frightened that not even a cart filled with money would persuade them to set foot in the mine again.

Those who turned from staunch skeptics to true believers following unexplainable sightings shared their frightening stories with others throughout the township and neighboring areas. These stories of strange lights and mysterious animal figures wandering in the night led many people in the Greater Akron area to stay inside their homes after dark.

Today, the coal mine is long gone. Its location is now occupied by Breitenstein Park. Shaneman's small house has long since vanished as well. It likely stood along the eastern side of Thirty-first Street Southwest near where it meets Eastern Road. There are no recent reports of a strange beast prowling the streets, but what of the red ghost light? Perhaps if you find yourself along Eastern Road some late night, you might still catch a glimpse of it floating through the fields. It may still point the way to Shaneman's buried fortune.

MARY CAMPBELL
AND THE LENAPE INDIANS

Many of you may have learned about Native Americans early in school; the various tribes and cultures were found across North America. These clans lived here for thousands of years, but once the white settlers reached the eastern coast of the United States, the Indians were pushed westward. Tempers flared between both the natives (who felt that the land belonged to them) and the European settlers (who thought that they had a right to the land instead of the "savages"), but the angry feelings also caused issues and turmoil between the various tribes of Indians. Such discontent and warring happened right here in what is now Akron and Summit County.

The Leni-Lenape (or Delaware) nation lived on the East Coast for thousands of years, according to archaeological record. By the early eighteenth century, the Dutch and English had swindled them out of their land and forced the tribes westward into Pennsylvania. It was here where forces collided and gave birth to a legendary kidnapping.

In 1758, a settler by the name of Campbell lived with his family on the banks of Canncoquin Creek in Cumberland County's Tuscarora Valley. Their neighbors—the Stuart family—lived at a nearby farm. One day, Mrs. Stuart took a trip to visit a distant neighbor, entrusting her children to the care of the red-haired and freckled ten-year-old Campbell daughter. When she returned, Mrs. Stuart heard her children screaming. As she neared the house, a party of Lenape Indians rushed out the front door with the household prisoners in tow, including her infant and their babysitter, Mary Campbell. The tribe captured Mrs. Stuart as well and headed for their camp in what is now Armstrong County, Pennsylvania. According to an account from General Lucius V. Bierce, the natives soon grew tired of the Stuart baby, and they "dashed out its brains in presence of its mother." One of Mrs. Stuart's children, a little seven-year-old boy named Sammy, was so exhausted during the trip that he couldn't walk another step to save his life. For three days, the Indians carried him on their backs. On the third day, the Lenape responsible for carrying Sammy fell behind the group of natives and prisoners, but he soon caught up without the child. As he came closer, Mrs. Stuart recognized the curly locks of hair hanging from his belt. Poor Sammy had been scalped.

The remainder of the trip to camp was quite a miserable journey for Mrs. Stuart. But throughout the ordeal, she, Mary and the rest of the young prisoners began to adapt to life with the Indians. The only documentation of the experience came from later recollections of Mary Campbell herself. The story, as she told it, goes that she gained the fatherly love of the tribe's chief and (as was common practice among the Native Americans of that period) was adopted by Chief Netawatwees, leader of the Turtle Clan of the Lenape nation.

The native custom of kidnapping and adopting white children and women primarily was caused by their own dwindling numbers during the mid- to late 1700s. There were many causes of death for the Indians during this time, but the main reasons were war and European diseases to which they had no natural immunity. In 1600, the Delaware population may have been as high as twenty thousand people, but within the span of one hundred years, several tribal wars and at least fourteen separate epidemics reduced their population to about four thousand. The worst time was between 1655 and 1670 when they lost 90 percent of their people.

After a fair amount of trouble with some other Pennsylvania tribes, Chief Netawatwees met with the chiefs of the Wyandot nation and told them of the wrongs suffered by him and his people. The chiefs advised Netawatwees that he should take his tribe and settle farther west on the Cuyahoga River (in present-day Ohio), leaving open the Muskingum and Big Beaver Rivers for the Wyandot. The chief took the advice, and shortly thereafter, Netawatwees and his Turtle Clan started across western Pennsylvania. They sought refuge at a series of large waterfalls along the Cuyahoga River in the fall of 1758. The falls were formed by three vertical descents of twenty-two, eighteen and sixteen feet.

According to Virginia Chase Bloetscher's *Indians of the Cuyahoga Valley and Vicinity*, "There were two villages at Big Falls, about where the Ohio

The dedicated Mary Campbell Cave. *Photo by Jeri Holland, 2008.*

Edison Dam is now—a Lenape village under Chief Net-a-wat-wees on the north side of the River and an Iroquois camp on the south side." When the Lenapes first arrived, they found a village of Iroquois on the south bank of the river, so they wintered in the cliffs on the northern side. The sheltered rock alcove was created during the last twelve thousand years when the Cuyahoga River was forced to carve a new path toward Lake Erie, when it was blocked by glacial debris. Far below, the Cuyahoga ran through a series of rapids about two miles in length. The stone alcove of the cliff face offered additional protection. A spring at the side of the alcove provided fresh water, and there was plenty of meat to be found in the forest and river. Here the tribe lived until they built a more permanent fort above their cliff dwelling.

Once they created their permanent village of *Lenapehoking* (or "Lenape Land"), they did not live in teepees but rather in wigwams or longhouses made of bark. First, a wooden framework was built, usually in a rectangular or oval shape, which was then covered with large sheets of bark. In the summer months, the houses were sometimes covered with reed mats. The village was composed of northern and southern sections. Houses to the south were mainly built for a single family, while the northern bark houses were larger, rounded, multiple-family structures where several related families usually lived together.

Bloetscher mentioned that "records [indicate]…there were two white captives living at the Delaware village of Chief Netawatwees on the River, near the site of the present Ohio Edison dam." So Mary lived, played and worked along the Cuyahoga River at Big Falls, spending her preteen and teenage years not far from the alcove (or "cave") where the Lenape spent the first winter. She went on living her life with the tribe, never knowing that in October 1764 her father placed an advertisement in the *Pennsylvania Gazette* asking for someone to bring his little red-headed girl home to him.

Though Mary was missed by her family, children were considered valued members of Lenape society. They were loved and well cared for while they helped out with family chores. Some of Mary's daily tasks included housekeeping and gardening. Still, she also had plenty of time to play; many Native American games helped tribal children build the skills they would need later in life. Mary and her Indian sisters played house with dolls made of leather, wood and cornhusks. They also played the "cup and pin game." In this game of skill, a hollow bone (or a piece of hard leather with a hole through it) was tied to a pin with a short string. The bone or leather piece was tossed into the air, and the player tried to put the pin through the hole.

Dancing accompanied by music and singing was a favorite pastime for the tribe. Mary listened to hide-and-water drums, bird bone whistles and wooden flutes played by the Lenapes, along with rattles made of turtle shell, bark and gourds. She and her Native American siblings were told exciting stories as a fun way to pass the time. They looked forward to long winter evenings by the fire, listening to the tales told by the elders. But these stories also served a serious purpose; legends and tales explained native beliefs about creation and social values and preserved historic past events, making storytelling an important part of a child's upbringing.

This peaceful life went on for several years, until Chief Netawatwees and the Turtle Clan fled south in 1764 to avoid Pontiac's War. They truly regretted leaving their peaceful haven at Big Falls; the Lenapes relocated to Newcomerstown along the lower Tuscarawas River. Soon, the battle was over and a peace treaty signed. With this treaty came a promise from the natives to release any white prisoners.

At the age of sixteen, Mary Campbell was returned to a European settlement in November 1764 during the famous release of captives

Depiction of Mary Campbell near the cave shortly after she arrived to the Big Falls. *Illustration by John Holland.*

orchestrated by Colonel Henry Bouquet at the close of Pontiac's War. Family tradition among Mary Campbell's descendants indicates that she was, at least at first, unhappy with being separated from the Lenapes. Historical records state that about half of the captives turned over to Colonel Bouquet attempted to return to their native kidnappers, a development that reportedly puzzled both the army and the communities to which the captives were being returned.

Being uprooted from her Lenape family and torn from her Indian brothers and sisters was just as traumatic for Mary as when she first was taken from her white family at ten years of age. Now closer to adulthood, it is likely that Mary dreamed of starting her own Lenape family and had planned delightedly on being a warrior's wife all her remaining years. She may even have had her eye on a handsome young native. Returning to her former life crushed these dreams forever. The rest of her life would be very different from those magical times at Big Falls.

Today, Chief Netawatwees stands watch over the city of Cuyahoga Falls in the form of a twenty-six-foot-tall carving on an island of land across from River Front Park. The carving is the handiwork of local resident Joe Frohnapfel and was dedicated on July 5, 2004.

The rock shelter where Mary Campbell and the Lenapes wintered in 1758 can still be found in Cuyahoga Falls along a hiking trail in Gorge

The gorge overlooking the Big Falls. It was not only explored by Mary Campbell, but Libertine Dixon mentioned that he killed a man in this area, as well. *Photo by Jeri Holland, 2008.*

Metro Park. For many years, it was known as Old Maid's Kitchen, until the Daughters of the American Revolution renamed it Mary Campbell Cave. A small plaque in the center of the cave gives visitors the story of her capture by Native Americans.

The thoughts and memories of life with the Lenapes may have stayed with Mary the rest of her life, as well as in her afterlife. Numerous times, a young red-headed girl has been witnessed running down the paths leading to the river. Some visitors have heard whistling and childlike singing—like someone tending to chores—in the early morning hours. About one hundred yards past the stone shelter of Mary Campbell Cave, a small group of children have been spotted playing a game around the trees. When a witness approaches the children, they suddenly vanish and are nowhere to be found. Could it be Mary still playing with her Indian siblings?

The Summit County metro parks allow hiking on the Gorge Trail from 6:00 a.m. until sunset. The trail is a beautiful place for a morning walk with family or friends. If you go there at dawn, maybe you, too, will catch a glimpse of Mary and her Lenape brothers and sisters or hear the echoes of her cheerful whistling from more than 250 years ago.

A Murderous Squaw

While Mary lived above the cave at the Big Falls, an Indian papoose—or child—was murdered. Suspicion was cast on an old woman of the tribe; other members of the Lenape looked down on her because of her assumed guilt. Still, there was not enough proof to convict her. Not long after the baby was killed, an Indian woman was murdered while working in a cornfield north of the Cuyahoga River settlement, just below present-day Cuyahoga Falls. Again the crime was blamed on the same old squaw, yet there was still too little proof against her for the tribe to prosecute her.

A year later, a Christian Native American preacher came along, attempting to convert the natives to the new faith. He carried with him two simple paintings: one pictured the narrow road to the "good place," to which very few people were traveling; the other was of a wide road showing many people headed to a "bad place." The preacher stopped short in the middle of his lesson to the Indians on heaven and hell. He stared directly at the old woman in horror and, with a shrill voice, exclaimed, "She is a murderer!"

The tribe grew wide-eyed in shocked amazement; they became loud and confrontational toward the accused old woman. The confirmation of their belief that the old woman was guilty grew so strong that they drove her from the settlement. The old woman, fearing for her life, had no choice but to travel west into the Cuyahoga Valley, but her reputation unfortunately—or fortunately, if she was, in fact, a killer—preceded her. She was captured there by another tribe of natives, who put her to trial and convicted her as a witch. At the time, the natives believed that anyone guilty of witchcraft should be condemned and killed—treated in the same manner as the white Christian settlers treated their accused witches. At the end of the trial, the old Indian woman was sentenced to be hanged at a makeshift gallows built by the natives. The gallows was formed by placing a pole across the divided, Y-shaped trunks of two trees, where the accused was suspended by the

Illustration by John Holland.

neck from a rope until death. While her suspected crimes took place on the outskirts of Akron, the woman's execution took place on the bank of a creek near Hinckley, thirteen miles northwest of the city. She was buried in a traditional style with her silver brooches and wristlets, with a kettle and cooking equipment for her to use in the afterlife.

Fifty-three years later, early settlers in Richfield, Ohio, unearthed her remains and stole her silver trinkets and kettle. Although it isn't known for sure what they did with the old woman's bones, it was believed that she was reburied in an old cemetery somewhere in this area. It is believed that she haunts the cemetery, still looking for the goods that were stolen from her.

Other squaws were accused of witchcraft and hanged in the area, too. According to historian Henry Howe, an eclipse of the sun occurred on June 17, 1806. The event, not widely understood to be the moon merely passing briefly over the sun, caused great fear and terror among both the settlers and Indians throughout Ohio. Those living in the Akron area were especially frightened. Some of the native women—possibly influenced by more educated settlers—tried to calm the tribesmen by saying that it was just a natural occurrence. The Indian men were not convinced; they accused the foretelling women of witchcraft and put them to death.

When the sun was completely hidden, the terrified Indians gathered together and formed a circle, marching around as each one fired his gun in the air to make as much noise as possible in order to frighten away the "evil spirit" threatening to destroy the world. One man of the tribe fired off his rifle at the same moment as the moon's shadow slowly lifted away from the sun; he was hailed as having driven away the evil spirit and given the role of tribal chief.

THE PHANTOMS OF RIVER STYX

O ver the years, a seventy-five-foot-tall steel railroad trestle outside of Medina, Ohio, has been the focus of a terrific legend. A ghost train is said to reenact its fatal plunge into the west branch of the Rocky River along River Styx Road at the site. However, the trestle does not deserve its haunted reputation. The story of the real haunted railroad bridge comes from well-documented events that occurred west of Akron, Ohio, more than a century ago in the tiny city of Rittman.

Situated in the northeastern edge of Wayne County, Rittman began as a little pioneer community on the Ohio frontier in the early 1810s, much like many other Ohio towns. It has been called Ellio and Arkona—the last name, being too similar to nearby "Akron," didn't last very long. The Atlantic and Great Western (later known as the New York, Pennsylvania and Ohio) Railroad came through town in 1871. The Baltimore and Ohio followed in 1881. At that time, the town was named after the treasurer of the NYP&O Railroad, Fredrick E. Rittman. Following bankruptcy, the NYP&O was bought out by the Erie Railroad in 1889.

Railroads helped shape Rittman and made the little town prosper. Salt deposits were discovered in 1897; E.J. Young capitalized on this and founded Wayne Salt (later called Ohio Salt; it became Morton Salt in 1948, which is still in business today). By then, Rittman was a cluster of fifty houses, a tile works, the salt factory, three stores, a post office, a blacksmith shop, a church, a schoolhouse and two railroad depots.

While Rittman never made a bid for notoriety, it possessed "that one thing that very few communities would desire," according to the *Cleveland Leader* in

1902. That "possession" was a phantom passenger train on the Erie track from Wadsworth that would appear during the night, wreck at the bridge over River Styx one quarter mile east of the depot and then disappear into thin air. But all of this started on that fateful day of March 22, 1899.

Engineer Alexander Wallace Logan had worked on railroads since he was nineteen. Originally from Scotland, Wallace worked his way up from track construction to locomotive engineer—a post he held for thirty-one years. Yet he felt that his days were numbered. Just two weeks earlier, he had told his coworkers that he knew he would meet his death on his engine.

Train No. 5, the Erie Limited, left Wadsworth with Wallace at the throttle that spring day carrying a fair number of passengers, many of whom were from Akron. The train, fueled by shovels of coal fed into the firebox by Byron Ward, thundered along the tracks traveling nearly eighty miles per hour. As the Erie Limited reached the small bridge across River Styx just outside Rittman at 7:30 a.m., something went horribly wrong. Ward, the fireman, later told reporters what happened from his point of view:

> I was standing in the gangway between the tank and the engine…when I felt the engine go off on the ties. I knew something was up and that we might have to jump. Just as she went off the rails, I saw Logan put on the emergency air, but I don't believe any four men could have reversed her running at that speed. I kept my eyes on Logan after he had put on the emergency, thinking I would jump if he did. But he didn't—he kept his hand on the throttle, and the last I saw of him he was leaning out the window, his teeth set with that firm determination so peculiar to him… calm and determined to do all in his power to save the lives of those on the train.

A drive rod had snapped, derailing the locomotive. Though Engineer Logan tried heroically to gain control, the speeding engine proved too powerful. The No. 5 suddenly jumped its tracks and turned over, followed by the baggage car and three passenger cars. Ward either jumped or was thrown from the train, causing serious injuries. Only five other people were mildly hurt. Wallace Logan was the only fatality. When they found his body in the twisted wreck of the locomotive, his hand was still clutched tightly to the throttle. It was Logan's decision to stay on the train and steer the engine that saved the lives of everyone on board.

Since that terrible morning, a ghostly train was observed and described by prominent, credible people from the area. "HAUNTED River Styx

Bridge—Fearful Sights Witnessed at the Place Where Engineer Logan Lost his Life," blared the headlines of the October 27, 1899 edition of the *Wadsworth Banner*. "Several Rittman people are very much excited at what has occurred at the Styx Bridge over the Erie at that place during the past week, and what they term was the appearance of a phantom train."

Just seven months after the accident on October 21, Wayne County coroner Dr. William Faber and a friend were traveling along Rittman Road at about 11:00 p.m. The doctor had been out visiting a patient. As he leisurely drove home, his attention was captured by the chugging of a fast-approaching train. Dr. Faber stood casually by the tracks to watch the train pass. Both Dr. Faber and his companion could see its blazing headlight and dense coal smoke belching from the stack.

As the train reached the bridge, the men heard the whistle's scream as the engine was thrown in reverse. *Clunk. Shunk.* Streaks of fire and sparks shot from the wheels of the train as it sped down the grade. Clouds of dust and smoke enveloped the locomotive, flames shot in every direction and huge clouds of steam hissed and erupted from the massive crash. Above the groaning timbers and breaking iron bars, Dr. Faber could hear the shrieks of passengers pinned beneath the wreckage. Awestruck at the horror, Faber and his friend raced toward the railroad tracks to save the victims within the overturned cars. Terror gave way to shock when they reached the bridge and found only quiet stillness—no train and no wounded people on the tracks. The River Styx below was still, without so much as a ripple on the calm surface.

The men hurried into town and told the townspeople of their experience, but not one soul would return to the site with them. Ever since the wreck of the Erie Limited, the citizens of Rittman had been terrified to pass near those railroad tracks after nightfall for fear of encountering a ghost.

Two years later, the *Akron Daily Democrat* announced the return of the ghost train: "Again the Erie's phantom passenger train has been seen near Rittman and the inhabitants of that town are now in a condition bordering on hysteria in consequence. The Erie's ghostly train is No. 5 that was wrecked two years ago on a trestle over the River Styx near Rittman."

The phantom train was again seen in mid-April 1901 by three upstanding citizens: J.B. Ewing, Amos Goldner and a man by the last name of Fielding. The trio was out for a late-night walk along the tracks near the trestle when they were startled by a loud locomotive whistle behind them. They turned in time to see the headlight of an approaching train from the direction of Wadsworth. Moonlight reflected off the plumes of black smoke billowing from the smokestack. The men thought it was the No. 1, running late and rushing down the track to make up time, and stepped off the rails patiently to let it pass. As the train rounded a slight curve, they could plainly see the baggage and mail cars; light poured from the windows of the three passenger coaches.

The train reached the trestle, where it whistled shrilly and slammed on the breaks, sparks flying from the locked wheels. All of the sudden, the locomotive dived off the trestle and plunged into the creek. There was a crackle of broken timbers, the hiss of steam and shrieks and groans from the trapped passengers. The threesome stood for a moment in astonishment before breaking into a run, hurrying down the embankment to the edge of River Styx. When they reached the water, there was no train to be found. The timbers of the trestle above them were stable and intact. It was as quiet as death. The three men hurried from the haunted bridge and ran into town. Surely it was just a hallucination. But a few local residents ran from their houses to meet the men. They had heard the accident as well and asked if there was anything they could do to help.

Some residents started to believe that the appearance of the ghost train was a warning, foretelling of an imminent disaster that would strike the village. But nothing happened except for more sightings of the ghost train. Any time that a prominent citizen witnessed the phenomenon, it was posted in the local papers. The frenzy of attention brought with it a forgotten ghostly tale that predated the railroad. W.J. Swisher, editor of the *Wadsworth Banner*, sent the *Akron Daily Democrat* an interesting story of another phantom near Rittman's River Styx Bridge. This time, the ghostly visitor took the romantic form of an Indian maiden hunting for her murdered lover.

Before the first white settlers pushed westward into what is now Wayne County, the valley near Rittman was home to the Chippewa tribe. The woods were filled with deer, bear, foxes, wolves and wildcats; plentiful creeks were traversed by canoes carrying natives to and fro. The River Styx was far larger than it is today, connecting to the mighty Tuscarawas River and the Portage Lakes. It was here in this lush valley that the Chippewas spent their summers in peaceful harmony with nature. An elder chief had a lovely daughter who was in love with a young warrior, to whom she was promised to marry. She would paddle her canoe along the River Styx, singing songs of her love.

One year, as the tribe made their way from the Portage Lakes to their summer campsite, they were ambushed by a group of Delaware, Choctaw and Mingo Indians. Many Chippewas were slaughtered—among them was the young brave engaged to the chief's daughter. So traumatized was the young girl that she went mad, deserting her tribe and vanishing into the wilderness. No one knows what happened to the young maiden, for she was never heard from again.

The *Akron Daily Democrat* recalled the rest of this sad tale and the experiences of early settlers in Rittman:

> *There was a tradition among the Chippewa that the spirit of this maiden had returned to the creek at midnight on the night of the 21st of October each year since 1821. So strongly had this tradition gained ahold upon these Indians that they could not be induced to go near that portion of the Styx during October.*
>
> *It was on the night of October 21, 1827, two young men decided to test the truth of this Indian tradition, so they set out from the mouth of the Styx north until they reached the spot a little north of where the railroad bridge now stands…Precisely at 12 o'clock there shot out from the opposite side of the stream, or pond, it was then, a bark canoe, bearing a headlight, such as was used by hunters in those days, in its bow, while in the stern sat a beautiful Indian maiden of about 20…The canoe glided around over the pond like a bird until the third time when it entered the channel and shot down the stream. The two young men breathlessly watched the canoe as its headlight began to disappear down the creek when the spell was broken by the low, plaintive Indian death song coming up the channel from the direction taken by the phantom. Suddenly the canoe shifted around and glided back toward the center of the pond… turned bottom upward and all disappeared together, and the young men were left alone in the blackness of the night, trembling in every nerve and lost little time in getting to their homes.*

Why is this area so haunted? Is it the softly flowing water or the horrid history? In Greek mythology, the River Styx (meaning "river of hate") was one of five rivers that surrounded the underworld. It separated life from the afterlife and had to be crossed by ferry upon death. Did whoever named this creek "River Styx" know something we don't?

All records show that the location of the actual train accident, the phantom train and the ghostly Indian maiden is near Rittman, Ohio. The real haunted River Styx Bridge is far smaller than the steel trestle near Medina. The abandoned Erie Railroad tracks cross River Styx along East Ohio Avenue half a mile northeast of Rittman near Martin Fritz Memorial

Park. Across Ohio Avenue, just north of the bridge, sits a small pond. This very well might be the site where the ghostly young Indian woman was last seen in her canoe.

I have shared these stories with you in order to correct the location and point you in the right direction. As always, please be respectful of the area and the people around you if you venture out for a visit. Please tell us about your adventures and share with us your photos and EVP by sending them to hauntedakron@gmail.com.

THE HISTORIC PORTAGE PATH

North of the city of Akron, you can find Ohio's oldest road: Portage Trail. Originally called the Portage Path (as it is still named west of the city), it may very well be one of the oldest highways west of the original colonies of the United States, having been the route of buffalo across Ohio. The old Portage Path extends between the Tuscarawas and Cuyahoga Rivers in Summit County, running a length of eight miles as surveyed in 1797 and 1806. A final survey for the Connecticut Land Company, completed by the second expedition sent out in 1897, showed the Portage Path's length being eight miles, four chains and fifty-three links (or 8 miles, 299 feet). In the spring, while the Little Cuyahoga was raging with water, the path was significantly shortened to just one mile. The path left the Cuyahoga River at the old Portage, continued about three miles north of Akron, ascended to higher ground to the west, turned south paralleling the Ohio and Erie Canal to Summit Lake and then continued south to the Tuscarawas River about a mile above the New Portage.

The importance of Portage Path varied over many years throughout history. When white settlers first moved to the area, they discovered the Indians using this trail as part of a common route between Lake Erie and the Ohio River. It was used to mark part of the legal boundary between the Six Nations to the east and the Western Indians. Although they were separated on land, both tribes used the same rivers and path for transportation.

In January 1785, representatives of the United States government met with the Indians (including the Wyandot, Delaware, Chippewa and Ottawa

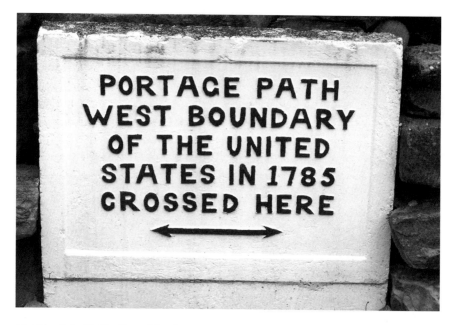

Outside of the Perkins Stone Mansion property was the Portage Path. *Photo by Rodney Johnson.*

nations) at Fort McIntosh, where the Ohio and Beaver Rivers joined together. During this meeting, the tribes surrendered all claims to the land east of the Cuyahoga and Muskingum Rivers in the Ohio Country as a part of what was called the Treaty of Fort McIntosh. At that time, the Portage Path became one of the boundaries of the newly formed United States of America. Other treaties were made in 1789 and 1795; they also designated the Portage Path and Cuyahoga River as the western boundary of the United States.

In September, during the first year of the War of 1812, a camp was established by General Elijah Wadsworth at the "Upper Headquarters," located at the old Portage. This post was of great importance throughout the war. Lake Erie marked one of the boundary lines during the war between Canada (then a British colony) and the United States. On account of this, General Wadsworth's soldiers did not follow the lakeshore from Cleveland to Huron; instead, they traveled up the Cuyahoga as far as the old Portage Path. There, ships for the war were built at old Portage and floated down to Lake Erie in 1813. Two of these vessels, the *Portage* and the *Porcupine*, played major roles in the remarkable naval victory achieved by Commodore Oliver Hazard Perry (the "Hero of Lake Erie") on September 10, 1813.

Evidence of the path's location was plainly visible for many years after its original followers faded into the retreating forests. The trail near Akron is still notably marked by a candelabra-shaped tree manipulated by the Indians and referred to as the Signal Tree. The path was very winding (a characteristic of all Indian trails), avoiding hills wherever possible and inching up around them when required. Today, the remains of the old footpath cannot be seen, but a five-mile section is followed closely by a wide, paved road called Portage Trail. If you ignore the twenty-first-century surroundings when standing on the old Portage Path, you will find yourself surrounded by a history so deep it will shake you to your core. The Indian Trail—the great highway of nations—and the people associated with the path led us to consider how much energy and emotion may still exist in the area—energy that fuels the hauntings that still occur today.

There are three Portage Path hauntings I will share with you in this book, although I'm quite sure that there are many more that can be shared in a predicted *Haunted Akron* sequel. The first, having been mentioned earlier, is the Signal Tree.

THE INDIAN SIGNAL TREE

Signal trees (sometimes known as "trail trees") are trees that have been altered by humans to grow into certain shapes to serve as identifiable "signals" marking trails, hide-outs, portages, tribal territories, sacred places and so on. They were formed by bending a sapling and securing it in place until the curve was set permanently as the tree grew. Oaks (especially white and red oaks) and other hardwood trees were most commonly used to make them. Most experts believe that the trees were manipulated into their shapes by Indians, who were known to do this to mark their trails. To fasten the curve, Native Americans bound the sapling using rawhide, sinew rope or stout vines.

The area around Akron and Summit County has a few signal trees. The one located on the Portage Path in Akron's Cascade Valley Park is said to be more than three hundred years old. Dubbed the "Indian Signal Tree" since the early 1800s, this burr oak is shaped like a candelabra or three-pointed fork. It stands more than one hundred feet tall and has an average branch spread of seventy-five feet. Signal Tree has a gigantic, four-foot trunk; at the very base, growing out horizontally on either side, are two enormous "arms." They grow symmetrically out to about thirteen feet from a sharp right angle and rise parallel on either side of the main trunk. This particular tree marks the exit point from the Cuyahoga River—the start of the Portage Path leading to the Tuscarawas River.

Here at the Indian Signal Tree, the supernatural experiences could best be described as a soft-flowing residual haunting. A residual haunting is a repetitive playback of the past, the images and/or sounds having been created by actions or events that were repeated many times. The energy spent by people in the area creates a psychic impression or energy "fingerprint." The apparitions encountered at sites of a residual haunting are not actual ghosts—they are recorded memories. These ghostly recordings will not notice or react to the living people around them. They are considered harmless and occasionally stop appearing naturally on their own as they fade away. Think of a stove; it stays hot for a long time after it shuts off. It's the same idea with residual haunts. Once the stockpiled energy dissipates, the playback (and hence the "ghost") is no longer around.

This was once the place the Indians entered/exited the Cuyahoga River. *Photo by Rodney Johnson.*

Many local ghost-hunting and paranormal groups have conducted investigations near the tree, with some positive results. Visitors have observed natives using the area surrounding the Signal Tree to enter the Cuyahoga River, as well as remove themselves, their gear and their canoes from the water. The river has since changed its course, and it no longer flows so closely to the tree. But the residual spirits are not aware of that, of course. If you sit quietly in the field within view of the tree on certain nights, you can still faintly see the images of the natives carrying the canoes above their heads at the end or beginning of their eight-mile portage. While standing near the entrance to the short trail at the parking lot, it is common for people to hear shuffling and rustling sounds around them, with no trace of any living person. Could this sound be an American Indian covering his canoe for his fellow tribesmen to use? Or are they the sounds of Indians quickly carving out a new canoe for the long journey to Lake Erie?

Cascade Valley Metro Park's Chuckery (or South) Area is located at 837 Cuyahoga Street, Akron, Ohio, 44303. It is open from 6:00 a.m. until 11:00 p.m.

THE PERKINS STONE MANSION

Farther south along the old Portage Trail, the mansion of Colonel Simon Perkins comes into view. Born in 1805 in Warren, Ohio, Colonel Perkins was the eldest son of General Simon Perkins. His father organized the Western Reserve Bank in 1813 and, along with Paul Williams, founded the town of Akron in 1825.

Colonel Perkins served in the Ohio legislature and was an active promoter of the Cleveland, Zanesville and Cincinnati Railroad. He purchased 115 acres of land adjacent to the Portage Path in 1832 for $1,300; on this land, Perkins had a glorious home built between the years 1835 and 1837. While the Perkins Mansion was under construction, he and his wife, Grace Ingersoll Tod, lived in a small wood-frame house nearby dating to about 1830.

The small house where Perkins first lived was rented to his business partner, the famed abolitionist John Brown, in 1844. The two men formed a wool enterprise called Perkins and Brown. The business had failed by 1849; the house (now greatly enlarged) still stands and houses the Summit County Historical Society. It is known today as the John Brown House.

Perkins Stone Mansion. *Photo by Carl Waite, 1934, courtesy of the Library of Congress.*

Perkins's new mansion was a fine example of the Greek Revival architecture that greatly influenced the design of many other homes and buildings during the early settlement of the Western Reserve. Built of native sandstone, with a two-story grand entrance, the Perkins Mansion was perched on a hill overlooking the city of Akron. The home and farm were a testimony to the family's prosperity. Perkins donated some of his own land for use as city parks. The oldest, named Grace Park in honor of his wife, was opened in 1844.

Today, the family home—Perkins Stone Mansion—is now a historic museum owned and operated by Summit County Historical Society. Surrounded by more than ten acres of beautiful grounds, the house contains items connected with the early history of Summit County. Situated near the mansion are the original well (dug through forty feet of sandstone), the original carriage house, a combination summer kitchen/laundry built in 1890 and the old woodshed, which now holds the visitor center.

Some of the mansion's original furnishings and dozens of items belonging to the colonel and his family are on display at the museum. These remaining artifacts combined with the museum's proximity to the historical Portage

Path are most likely some of the reasons why Perkins Stone Mansion is believed to be quite haunted.

When I paid a visit to the mansion, I found the house to be fascinating and full of history. Many of the rooms throughout the mansion provided ghostly stories experienced by visitors, employees and volunteers alike. People tend to avoid the first-floor bedroom that once belonged to Simon and Grace Perkins. It is highly unusual for a bedroom from that era to be on the first floor, so I asked the staff and discovered that Mrs. Perkins suffered from paralysis. Stairs became a great difficulty for her, and the bedroom was relocated downstairs. Within this bedroom is the original bed, with a rope frame that needs to be tightened from time to time. Although visitors and employees are not permitted to sit on the bed, fresh imprints appear on the feather mattress and quilt. The curator has needed to tighten the ropes a few times from its ghostly use; each time staff members enter the room, they have to straighten out the covers before leaving.

Colonel Simon Perkins married Grace Ingersoll Tod on September 23, 1832. She was the daughter of Judge George Tod and sister to David Tod, the twentieth governor of Ohio. Grace, along with her sisters Mary Tod Evans and Julia Tod Ford, established the Ladies Cemetery Association, an organization committed to keeping the Akron Rural Cemetery (now known as Glendale Cemetery) beautiful and well maintained. She continued to support this association until her death by helping to raise funds to beautify the cemetery, sponsoring entertainment in the form of concerts, picnics and other social events. It has been said of Grace that "few women in private life were more widely known or universally loved." After her death on April 6, 1867 (while visiting her son in Sharon, Pennsylvania), an Akron newspaper posted a notice asking for people to visit her one final time at her stone mansion. Simon followed on July 21, 1887, and was reunited with his wife in their plot at Akron Rural Cemetery.

Shortly after the death of Grace Perkins, a portrait of her was painted and hung in the mansion. Like many old paintings of the time, the eyes appear to follow you around the room, giving many visitors the strange, creepy feeling of being watched. But most people don't think it's a coincidence; they believe that Mrs. Perkins really is watching your every move and letting her opinions of people be known. Grace had an especially strong dislike for the previous director of Summit County Historical Society, most likely because both of them had strong, dominant personalities. However, Grace seems to have a greater preference for the current curator and director, Leianne Neff Heppner.

In the entry hall is a grand staircase leading you to the second floor. The ghosts of a woman and a small boy have been seen near the very top of the stairs. One of the few documented pieces of paranormal evidence at the house is a photograph taken of the staircase in 2005. A figure can be seen in the image; some say that it's a photo of the boy himself.

The young boy may not be the only phantom child at Perkins Stone Mansion. While the building was undergoing renovations, a man named Joel was working on a second-floor bedroom of the museum, discussing room arrangements with two decorators, when he heard a noise from the floor above. Climbing the stairs leading to the third floor to investigate, he came eye to eye with two small children—a boy and a girl—rolling a red-and-white alphabet ball back and forth to each other. Joel hurried back down to the first floor to tell Leianne what he had seen. When the director heard the description of the ball, she recognized it instantly. The exact same ball had been in the Perkins Collection and was being stored temporarily in the John Brown House until renovations were completed. Leianne retrieved the antique red-and-white ball from their collection. It was identical to the one seen by Joel. He returned to his work on the second floor but later felt that he was being watched. As Joel looked out through a door jam, he spotted the children peeking down at him from the stairs.

I did not see any ghosts during my own tour of the mansion; however, I did hear children giggling upstairs a few times. A school bus full of children had been at the museum when I arrived, but I swore that the children had left by the time I had reached the second floor.

During the 1980s, it was the responsibility of one staff member to make the house ready for tours each morning. In the kitchen was an old-fashioned highchair with a baby doll sitting in it. Nearly every morning, when flipping on the lights, the employee noticed that the doll had either been placed in a different position or had been moved entirely. Other staff insisted that they had never touched the doll. Was it the little girl and boy playing during the night?

The period kitchen was my favorite room of the entire house. The original fireplace looked ready to cook in, and there were even pans inside the bread oven that was built into the brick fireplace. Like other old houses, the kitchen was built as an extension off the house to keep the rest of the home cooler in summer and to contain a fire should one break out. But what captured my attention the most was the story of the ghost of an old Indian visiting the mansion's kitchen every so often.

Local historian Arthur H. Blower wrote about the ghostly native of Perkins Stone Mansion back in 1955. An old Indian man had been seen occasionally coming through the back kitchen door and sitting silently by the fireplace to warm himself. Half an hour later, he would walk out the same door without so much as a goodbye. Even after the Native Americans were pushed westward, some tribespeople took any opportunity to visit their friends—both alive and dead—in the vicinity. Staff members at the mansion have heard accounts of Indians secretly visiting the area after the mansion was built. Indians returned a number of times to visit the graves of their ancestors buried in a cemetery near the property of Simon Perkins; afterward, they would visit the mansion, partake in dinner and then rest. It was the family's custom to feed the natives in the kitchen at a table suspended by four iron rods from hooks in the ceiling. The table would be removed when the meal was finished, and the Indians would lie in front of the fireplace wrapped in their blankets and sleep through most of the evening. Today, the hooks in the ceiling can still be seen. Are the old Indians still making visits? Some members of the staff think so.

I strongly suggest a visit to Perkins Stone Mansion for any ghost hunter, investigator or just plain history buff. While there, ask to see the original ghost photo located in the foyer, and don't forget to look for the children. But be careful—Mrs. Perkins is watching.

Summit County Historical Society is located within and operates the Perkins Stone Mansion at 550 Copley Road in Akron, Ohio. Staff provide tours throughout the year, and luckily for you ghost hunters, they also provide such investigations during the season. The schedule can be found on the Haunted Akron website, www.hauntedakron.info.

SUMMIT LAKE SUICIDE

Near the southern end of the Portage Path is Summit Lake. From this point, water flows both north to Lake Erie and south to the Ohio River and, eventually, the Mississippi. Just in the last three hundred years, there were Native Americans who used the lake. Then, of course, the Europeans settled in the area, bringing with them the canal era, when the Ohio and Erie Canal passed right across the edge of the lake. The towpath, used by mules and fishermen alike, was made of floating wooden barges. In the late nineteenth century, two resorts were also established on Summit Lake. They featured picnic areas, baseball parks and bandstands; there were amusement parks, vacation cabins, fishing sprees and ice skating. Lakeside Park on the east did not offer alcohol, but Summit Lake Park on the west did, earning it the nickname "Beerside."

Reaching as far back as records were kept in Akron, there were hundreds of drownings—possibly even more—on Summit Lake. Lots of accidents; lots of deaths. And now, lots of ghosts. (It really can't be helped.) A ghost is best described as the spirit of an individual that, because of a traumatic or violent event, refuses to move on and remains behind after death. These spirits may also stay because of a strong emotional tie—love, anger or hate—even unfinished business. Composed of the energy of the deceased, these entities retain their appearance and personality, behaving as the people did in life. If someone was a good and caring person, their spirit will be the same. But if they were angry or cruel, then that is the trait that will remain with their specter.

There's a mix of both gentle and mean-spirited ghosts at Summit Lake. One of the most famous phantoms involves a tragic drowning and its victims, whom you might encounter on the lake even to this very day.

Emil Bergdorf was a tall, muscular and dark-complected thirty-six-year-old. He was employed by a mining company at the turn of the last century to drill wells and search for veins of coal. One day, while working at a job site in Cleveland, he met a woman who caught his eye and, smitten, soon began courting her. Emil bent down on one knee and asked his new lady to marry him and move with him to Akron. She gladly accepted. Emil had never been happier in his life. He was determined to make a good life for his future bride, but on the day of her arrival in Akron, she promptly changed her mind. She refused to marry Bergdorf, turned around and headed back to Cleveland. Emil was downright furious; he drank himself into a stupor and repeatedly threatened to kill himself over the next few weeks.

On Friday night, June 7, 1901, Bergdorf spent some time drinking away his sorrows at Beerside. When he was good and numb, he asked an employee from Lakeside Park, Newton Ramey, to take him across Summit Lake to Lakeside. Mr. Ramey complied, and the two men started rowing across the lake. Midway across, Bergdorf started shaking the boat from side to side, screaming that he wished he were dead. "I'll get myself a gun," Emil slurred, "and put a bullet in my brain just as soon as we reach Lakeside!"

Mr. Ramey shook his oar in Bergdorf's face. "I'll knock your block off if you don't sit still and quiet down!" Emil sank down and took a seat. They made it safely to Lakeside without another incident.

Late the next evening—after another whiskey-filled night at Summit Lake Park—Emil Bergdorf caught up with forty-nine-year-old Michael Shea and his friend Oliver Crosier, twenty-four, asking for a ride back to Lakeshore. The men could smell the booze on Emil's breath. With great reluctance, Michael allowed the fellow to join them in his small rowboat. Bergdorf sat quietly until they were in the middle of the lake, when he started rocking the boat until Michael and Oliver were successfully dumped overboard. It is not clear (even to this day) whether he changed his mind about committing suicide or wanted to murder someone before drowning himself. In any event, Bergdorf managed to take Crosier under the water with him. Oliver was a strapping young man but was no match for Bergdorf's strength.

Michael Shea later shared his personal account on June 10, 1901, with the *Akron Daily Democrat*:

> [F]*or the past three weeks I have been tending the cane stand at Lakeside Park. After business was over Saturday night, Ollie Crosier and I went across to Summit Lake. We were there but a little while and started back… and as soon as daylight came we would go fishing.*
>
> *Bergdorf hailed us as we were about to leave Summit Lake Park and wanted to come across. I knew the fellow slightly from having lately seen him around here, but told him I did not like to take so many in a small boat. He had been drinking, but was not so very drunk, and as he insisted we at last took him in. He sat in the stern. I was in the bow and Crosier at the oars.*
>
> *We had not gone far when Bergdorf began rocking the boat as though he were crazy.*
>
> *"Let up on that; you'll drown us," Crosier said, and I said the same.*
>
> *Very soon Bergdorf rocked the boat again and filled it half full of water. Crosier and I remonstrated and began bailing out with our hats. Bergdorf said he didn't care if he did drown, and suddenly leaning far over, upset the boat almost before we knew what he was about.*
>
> *We all pitched out and as I came right side up, Bergdorf, who was a big brawny fellow, got hold of me. Not being an expert swimmer, I saw at once we would both drown if Bergdorf held to me, and that it would be all off with us in this world, too, if I tried to struggle with the more powerful fellow. I let myself sink in the water, believing that if I could stay under*

longer than he could he would let go. That is what he did, and diving, I came up five feet away from him.

This had taken a great deal less time that it takes to tell it, and as I came up I saw Bergdorf have hold of Crosier's arm and shoulder. They were 20 feet from the boat which I now get hold of, and in the fog I could not make them out perfectly. They did not seem to be struggling, and Crosier may have been trying to get Bergdorf ashore. I called to them to get hold of the boat and we could paddle it along till help came or we reached land. But Crosier could do nothing with the heavier man hanging to him and I thought they went down together. Maybe they didn't. Crosier was a good swimmer and could have taken care of himself but for Bergdorf. It was very foggy. I did not know in which direction the nearest shore lay. Crosier did not know.

William Haynes, the night watchman, was on duty at Lakeside Park that night when he heard a cry for help at 12:40 a.m. The fog made it impossible to see more than twenty feet from the shore. Haynes boarded a small boat and pushed off from the towpath in search of the troubled craft. Another man, Park Bowman, stood watch from the path and kept in vocal contact with Mr. Haynes to help keep his bearings while looking for an overturned boat. After half an hour, Haynes found and rescued the exhausted, half-conscious Michael Shea. Unaware of the other two men in the water, he headed back for shore. It wasn't until 5:00 a.m. that the local undertaker was notified and began a search for the bodies.

Thousands of curious people came to Summit Lake upon hearing news of the drownings. Many men aided in the hunt for the two men who remained missing. No bodies floated to the surface, so Charles Tuttle Parks (the owner of Parks Undertaking Company), his employees and four policemen began using dynamite to loosen any corpse from the deep. They strung hooks on rope and dredged a space sixty feet wide across the lake. The fire department joined in, using four sets of grappling hooks and a long grappling pole.

Finally, on Sunday afternoon, Bergdorf's body was found in a thirty-foot-deep section of the lake some two hundred feet northeast of the Summit Lake Park boat landing. Akron firemen from Station No. 1 continued to look for young Crosier's body, but at 8:30 p.m. on Sunday, the hooks were brought in and the search was temporarily put on hold. Because his body wasn't found near Bergdorf, it was plausible that he didn't take the young man down with him. He may have managed to break free and swim some distance away, but the fog sitting atop the lake made finding the shore impossible. Crosier also had suffered from asthma.

Breathing trouble could have made him exhausted and confused. Shortly after resuming the search Monday morning, they discovered Crosier's body in another section of the lake.

It didn't take long—only a matter of a few hours—for recreationists to begin reporting seeing Emil Bergdorf and Oliver Crosier on the shores of Summit Lake. Some even spotted them in a rowboat near where both men lost their lives. Rumors spread that it was all a farce and that the men never actually drowned. It wasn't until those naysayers were able to view the bodies that they realized that the men they saw out on the lake weren't real. Today, more than one hundred years later, Bergdorf and Crosier can still be seen and felt in and around Summit Lake. If you take a rowboat out late at night, be sure to wear a life vest. Sometimes, boats will start rocking violently and filling with water for no reason whatsoever, even on the calmest nights. Other people occasionally witness a young man near the shoreline wheezing deeply and asking for help to save his friends in the water. When they go out looking for his friends in need of rescuing, they never find anyone—even the man asking for help has disappeared.

GHOSTS OF THE CIVIC THEATER

D owntown Akron holds a unique gem. Once home to many theaters and movie houses, only one of the old relics still stands. Wedged between façades is the Civic Theater with its bright neon marquee. Somehow it has stood the ravages of time and defied the wrecking ball. And for that, its ghosts are surely thankful.

Early in the twentieth century, this particular spot along Main Street was chosen for a vaudeville theater. It was to be called the Hippodrome. Only the front archway was built before the deal went bust. But another man soon came along with a grand vision for the site; his name was Marcus Loew.

Marcus "Max" Loew was born on May 7, 1870, in the Lower East Side of bustling New York City. He was an industrious young man, working hard at whatever job he could find. In 1899, Max made an attempt to venture into the business of real estate. Loew soon took notice of the "penny arcades" springing up around the country. He became a partner in the Automatic Vaudeville Company in the early 1900s. This marked the beginning of his interest in constructing theaters.

Max formed Loew's Consolidated Enterprises in 1910 and starting building arcades across the country. But silent movies were catching on— and films with sound, called "talkies," were under development—and Max wanted to get in on the action. His business eventually became Loew's Incorporated in 1919 and changed from small, coin-operated entertainment to movies. In 1920, Max purchased Metro Pictures Corporation. Four years later, he bought Goldwyn Picture Corporation, known for its trademark "Leo the Lion." His venture was joined by Louis B. Mayer within a year; the new company was called Metro-Goldwyn-Mayer (MGM). That same year, Max visited Akron and saw the Hippodrome archway on Main Street. He thought it would be the perfect spot to build a new theater.

His new Akron theater was unlike anything he had attempted before. It would be equipped not only for vaudeville performances but for talking motion pictures as well. But that wasn't the only advancement; it would be the first-ever theater with an air cooling system (or air conditioning, as we now call it). Construction of the Loew's Theater along Main Street proved to be a challenge. The land purchased for the building flanked the Ohio and Erie Canal. Since Akron still owned the waterway, the city refused to allow builders to destroy it. But Loew was a genius; his company purchased air rights above the canal and constructed the front lobby on cement piers directly over the water. It still runs beneath to this very day.

Marcus Loew, together with the renowned theater architect John Eberson, worked vigorously on designing the extravagant interior at the total cost of $2 million. Sadly, Marcus Loew never lived to see his project completed. Just two years into design and construction, Max passed away on September 5, 1927, in New York. Eberson continued his work, hand-selecting many of the fixtures and decorations on his travels far and wide.

The 3,500-seat theater was opened on Saturday, April 20, 1929, to a grand welcoming. A Spanish patio of Moorish influence, along with statues of Greek goddesses and cherubs and a picturesque Moorish monk, lent a glamorous atmosphere to the interior of the theater, "which is a glorious maze of brilliant colors, skillfully blended into one harmonious radiance" boasted the *Akron Topics*. It was a true atmospheric theater, popular throughout the Depression; the high dome of the auditorium, with its starlit sky and drifting clouds—hence the term "atmospheric"—pleased theatergoers and offered a short escape from reality. Everywhere there were hints of Morocco and other exotic lands. Best of all, opening day

Loew's Theater on Main Street in Akron. *Courtesy of Cuyahoga Falls Library.*

101

The Civic Theater stage after renovations. *Photo by Rodney Johnson, 2011.*

marked the screening of the 100 percent all-talking movie *The Voice of the City*, starring Robert Ames, Sylvia Field and Willard Mack. The newspapers estimated that at least ten thousand people attended during the afternoon and evening showings on the first day.

Going to Loew's Theater during the 1930s was a momentous occasion. It was a magical place, full of exciting sights and sounds. "I'll never forget the feeling I got the first time I walked inside the lobby and looked up," vaudeville dancer Art Kalmer recalled in a 1999 article for the *Akron Beacon Journal*. "I was awed. I couldn't believe it. It was so beautiful."

The Loew's Theater may have been the scene of a murder most *fowl*. For years, box office customers were greeted in the main entrance hall by a multicolored parrot named Loretta. Now, parrots are notoriously fickle creatures, known for their squawks as well as their bites. One customer reached a bit too close to Loretta, and the bird bit the hand. Shortly after the fiasco, the parrot died under what has been described as "mysterious circumstances." Loretta may not fly around the theater in the afterlife, but you can still see her today. Her taxidermied likeness sits quietly on its perch in a gilded cage in an alcove to the left of the grand staircase.

The Civic Theater on Main Street near Lock 3 Park. *Photo by Andrew Borgen.*

Over the years, the theater lost much of its glimmer. In 1965, local leaders created the nonprofit Community Hall Foundation to purchase and preserve the theater. That's when Loew's was renamed the Akron Civic Theatre. Nonetheless, the interior continued to decay and fall apart. However, in June 2001, the Civic was closed for extensive renovations, totaling more than $20 million. It was reopened in November the following year, restored to its former splendor. It is one of only five atmospheric theaters built during the Great Depression still standing in the United States.

Excitement, drama, energy—customers brought it all with them. For eighty-two years, this building has housed the imprint of these emotions night after night, day after day. It isn't surprising that when the lights go down and the people leave, residual echoes from the past still play on. No one should be surprised at encountering intelligent hauntings from the past, either. In this type of haunting, you are dealing with a manifestation that can communicate and interact with living people in a seemingly "intelligent" way. These ghosts are simply described as the personality of a person who once lived and who has stayed behind in our world.

Paranormal events have been experienced at the Civic Theater since the 1970s, and a number of legends have formed surrounding the theater since that time. One popular tale involves the ghost of "Fred the janitor," said to haunt the building. It's claimed that he worked there in the earliest days of Loew's and died in the building. Unfortunately, there are no records of any janitorial workers by that name. Employees are confused by the rumors; no stories of "Fred" float among them, but they have shared tales of a different man on whom this legend may have been based.

Paul Steeg, born on November 18, 1900, was an engineer who worked at the theater since opening day in 1929. He was passionate about his job and loved the theater; the place became his life's work—quite literally. Steeg would often joke with his coworkers, "I'll always be here. I'll come back [even after I'm dead]." He worked at the theater up until his death in Cuyahoga Falls on June 16, 1972. Since that day, staff members have wondered if his famous words had, in fact, come true.

Whenever anything strange happens in the theater, employees are quick to blame it on Paul. Some say it in jest, while others strongly believe it. People have reported a warm and friendly (yet somewhat watchful and protective) presence at the top of the grand staircase. Other strange feelings and unexplained activity in both the projection room and backstage area may also be attributed to the spirit of Paul, forever taking care of the place in which he spent most of the last forty-three years of his life.

Another Civic ghost is known as the "lady in white." She has been spotted infrequently in the basement dressing rooms, quietly weeping by herself. Her distraught apparition never lingers for long, and she hurries away when noticed. Her early 1800s attire may suggest that she predates the building and that she may actually be haunting the canal, mentioned earlier, that runs beneath the theater. According to local legend, a woman committed suicide by drowning herself in the canal long before the theater was built. It is her ghost, they say, that wanders the canal beneath the Civic and occasionally pays a visit to the basement.

A mysterious, well-dressed male spirit sporting a top hat has been seen backstage and in the balcony on several occasions. He is often called "the actor," and according to the legend, he was once an actor during the early days of vaudeville at the theater. Long-since dead, he can't resist a final desperate attempt to catch a hint of limelight. I have witnessed this particular apparition firsthand in broad daylight. While taking photographs of the Civic from Bowery Street for a history project, a close friend and I spotted a finely dressed man wearing a tuxedo and a top hat standing at an upstairs window looking out across Main Street. Perhaps he is still waiting for his audience to arrive.

THE SUBMARINER'S TRUNK

Wartime tragedy can be difficult to forget. Countless men and women from Ohio have died in battle since the Revolutionary War. Our cemeteries are strewn with the graves of fallen soldiers who never lived to see home again. One man from Akron, Patrick Paul Sullivan, was lost at sea almost seventy years ago. While his body never came home to rest in peace, his family believes that Paul may have returned from his watery grave.

Born in 1915 and raised in the Firestone Park neighborhood, Patrick Paul Sullivan's most valuable possession was his family. He was a loving man, an avid boxer and wrestler and his siblings always praised him highly and loved his sense of humor. Shortly after his 1933 graduation from Garfield High School, Paul headed to Cleveland, attempting to try his hand at becoming an undertaker. The job wasn't quite what Paul had hoped for and expected, so instead he joined the navy. During these military years, he didn't forget about his neighbor and (literally) girl-next-door sweetheart, Norma Jane Wolff. The two were married in 1940, just before the Second World War changed their lives completely.

After the Japanese bombed Pearl Harbor on December 7, 1941, the United States was dramatically pulled into the war. Paul was a pharmacy technician for the navy at the time and quickly went off to war. As pharmacist's mate first class (PHM1), he was assigned to a United States naval submarine named the USS *Grunion* (SS-216), named after a sleek silver fish found off the coast of California.

The USS *Grunion. Courtesy of the Library of Congress.*

After a performance test (called a "shakedown") off the coast of New London, Connecticut, the *Grunion* set sail for the Pacific Ocean on May 24, 1942. One week later, as the submarine traveled through the Gulf of Mexico on its way to the Panama Canal, it came to the aid of its comrades on the wreck of United States Army Transport (USAT) *Jack*, attacked by a German U-boat. The sailors rescued sixteen survivors and conducted a search for the thirteen crew members still lost at sea but came up empty-handed. The *Grunion* deposited its shipload of survivors on June 3 at the U.S. Naval Base at Coco Solo and continued on to Pearl Harbor.

After ten days of intensive training in Hawaii (June 20–30), the *Grunion* and its sixty-nine-member crew headed north toward the Aleutian Islands, arching between Russia and Alaska, for its first war patrol. The patrol started off the coast of Russia near Kiska Island, where the submarine sank two enemy patrol boats and survived an attack by a Japanese destroyer just north of the island. On July 30, the U.S. Navy received a radio transmission from the *Grunion* reporting severe antisubmarine activity near Kiska Harbor. The order was given for the *Grunion* to return to Dutch Harbor farther east toward mainland Alaska.

No reply ever came from the USS *Grunion.* There were no further transmissions from the vessel. Air and sea searches launched by the navy both in and around Kiska Island were unproductive. Paul Sullivan and his sixty-eight fellow crew members were never seen nor heard from again. The submarine was reported overdue from patrol; the incident was kept quiet, and family members weren't notified for two months. The *Grunion* was assumed lost by October 5. The crew was officially declared dead on August 2, 1943.

World War II came to an end in 1945. Shortly after the Allied victory, the U.S. Navy combed over Japanese records, but none of the documents showed antisubmarine attacks in the Kiska area. The navy submarine remained missing for sixty years until the sons of Lieutenant Commander Mannert L. Abele, the *Grunion's* skipper, stumbled across an account on the Internet in 2002 regarding an encounter between a Japanese troop transport and the submarine. A Japanese naval researcher, Yutaka Iwasaki, had discovered the firsthand account of a crew member from the Kano Maru who reported that the *Grunion* had torpedoed their boat. When the submarine surfaced to deliver the final shots, the Japanese ship opened fire and sank the *Grunion*. Brad, Bruce and John Abele assembled together a team of international underwater searchers and divers, which resulted in the discovery of the *Grunion* off the coast of Kiska Island in 2006. The mystery was finally solved. The sub had confronted a Japanese freighter before sinking, taking all sixty-nine lives on board with it.

Paul Sullivan may have gone down with his vessel, but it seems that his spirit found its way back to his old family home on Neptune Avenue. Back in 1942, just after Sullivan's death, Paul's parents, Basil and Florence Sullivan, received a delivery from the U.S. Navy. They had shipped back a wooden travel trunk containing his personal belongings. Still dealing with the grief from losing their son, the couple placed the trunk in the basement and forgot about it. The Sullivan family moved to California in 1969 and sold their home to Patti and Fred Christ.

The dusty old trunk was still sitting in the basement when the new owners purchased the unassuming Colonial-style suburban house. They checked out the trunk and then left it where they found it, unaware of the trunk's history—or that it came with its original owner, Paul Sullivan. It didn't take long for Pattie to start realizing that their house was haunted. Slowly, she started to catch tiny glimpses of Paul—or at least parts of him. His legs would appear in different parts of the house; sometimes they were attached to the rest of him. Patti even awoke on the couch one afternoon to see Paul lounging across from her on the love seat.

Over the years, her daughter, Dawn, and even her grandson have encountered Paul's apparition in his old family home. Paul is what paranormal investigators call an "intelligent haunting" because he is able to interact with the living. He has even called the grandson by name. Paul's presence never frightened any of the Christs; in fact, they all seem to accept him as a part of their family. After discovering his identity, Patti and Fred contacted the Sullivan family out west. They since have met and keep in contact with Stanley Sullivan—Paul's younger brother—and his family. The Sullivans were happy to know that their relative is content and happily back home; they decided that it would be best for his trunk to stay with him in Akron instead of being sent to California with his relatives. Both the Christs and Sullivans welcomed Paul's return and hope that he stays around; his trunk still sits in the basement.

If you live in a haunted house, it may be frightening at first. A stranger in your home may be an uncomfortable feeling, but remember: you might be the real stranger. If you find out why the ghost or spirit is around, you just might be more accepting of having an additional disembodied family member around.

HISTORICAL GHOSTS

Summit County Beacon April 11, 1877

A REAL GHOST—KENT HAS A GHOST

It may not be a real ghost, although they say it is. It appears that eight years ago, a woman now living in Kent, assisted in dressing another woman for the grave (the last named woman was dead). Last Saturday night, just after the first mentioned woman had gone to bed, the ghost of the dead woman appeared at the bedside of the live woman, clothed in the very raiment she (the dead woman) had been buried in. The live woman jumped out of bed and started down stairs. She had gone half way when she fainted and fell the remaining distance to the bottom. The above is the story of the live woman.

Summit County Beacon April 27, 1881

A GHOST AT THOMASTOWN [EAST AKRON]

Thomastown has a ghost. Henry Craft, who boards in the old house just east of the Baptist Church, claims to have seen on Monday night, the spirit of J.X. Evans, who died in the house about eight years ago. Sam Stall, another boarder, backs this up with the assertion that not long since he saw two ghostly hands above him in the middle of the night. Strange noises are also reported, such as knocks, poundings, etc. Two other houses in the vicinity are also reported haunted. So go the stories, at any rate.

Summit County Beacon, December 25, 1878

THE STRANGE CAVORTING OF A SILVER STREET GHOST

In the western part of the city, in small frame house accessible only by a tortuous footpath striking off to the north from West Market street, and leading beside a deep ravine, live a widow and two daughters, busy, hardworking bodies, all of them, but as the story will show, inclined somewhat to the superstitious. The fact is, the little antique structure in which they reside is reported to be haunted by some mysterious sprite which only manifests itself in the dead hours of the night; and that in the most terrifying modes imaginable.

One night last week, the old lady was awakened by the deep, painful, prolonged breathing of some one evidently in his death throes, and from the best service which her eyes could give her, judged by the affrighted women to be ensconced directly behind her stove. Presently this manifestation ceased and the sprite by way of diversion playfully gamboled about the room, spinning about at lightning speed and winding up by mounting upon the bed and reclining upon the feet of the terrified occupants. Later it passed its ghostly hands upon their faces, cavorted for a brief season about the walls and ceiling and at last retired, leaving the unprotected trio to resign themselves again to Morpheus, as speedily as the harrowing recollections of the dread manifestations would permit. For five consecutive nights these visitations continued, slightly varied with the occasion but essentially similar. That the sprite was possessed of a weakness for "apple juice" was demonstrated beyond question, on one night in particular, when a huge cider barrel was made to tumble from its accustomed position to minister to its depraved appetite.

These occurrences are not readily explained by the mystified residents on Silver street, and as may readily imagined they are "all torn up" over the affair. As far as we are informed, the Metzler family have not moved into the same neighborhood, but it is rumored among the knowing ones that the stone-slinging ghost of "Hell's Half Acre" has become convinced that better material to work upon might be found in the more romantic gullies and ravines in which our western outskirts abound, and has recently taken up his abode there.

Akron Daily Democrat, July 29, 1899

GHOSTLY PHOTOGRAPH: STRANGE IMAGE OF A MAN SEVERAL YEARS DEAD

Joseph Jeanes, a man past 70 years of age, whose integrity is above reproach, is responsible for one of the strangest stories that ever came out of the mysteries of a photographer's dark room.

On his oath he states that while he was developing a plate a few days ago the ghostly outline of a man long dead appeared upon the negative beside the picture of the man he had photographed, who, being a friend of the dead man, recognized him immediately.

Mr. Jeanes has taken his affidavit to the truth of the picture, and as he comes from good Quaker stock it will be accepted.

This is how the ghost appeared in the picture: A man who gave his name as Burnes went to Jeanes' establishment to have a photograph taken. Burnes, who is an athlete, had the picture taken in his athletic togs. The use of the

Ghost photos in Akron? *Illustration by John Holland.*

usual acids failed to remove it from the plate, and the exposure was made and the plate was being developed when something white appeared upon the negative mixed in with the background. At a loss to know what it was Mr. Jeanes threw the plate away.

A second exposure was made, and the same mysterious shadow appeared upon it.

The same shadow appeared like a fatal stain upon the third exposure, but in a less marked degree, and Jeanes decided to print it. He told Burnes to call for the finished pictures in a few days.

Burnes called and when the pictures were handed to him he looked at the first one and exclaimed: "Good heavens! How did that get there?"

"I am as much at loss to account for it as you are," replied Jeanes. "My dark room is all right. My developer is good. That never happened to me before in all my experience."

"It's my trainer," shouted Burnes, still fearfully agitated.

"Your trainer?" repeated Jeanes blankly.

"And he has been dead four years!" cried Burnes, dropping the photograph in dismay and retreating toward the door.

"Come in tomorrow and we'll try again to see if the same thing appears," solicited the photographer.

"Not if I know myself," replied Burnes, "You couldn't get me into that studio of yours again with a team of mules." He then darted out of the door and down the street as if an army of spirits were after him.

CONCLUSION

At the beginning of this book, I pondered for quite some time what I wanted to accomplish. My main goal was not only to offer historical and current hauntings but rather to show that each haunting offers a documented history behind it, as well. Akron and the surrounding communities offer rich history and an unending array of hauntings to research and explore. Ghost hunting and history go hand in hand, as any serious paranormal researcher will tell you. The paranormal and history *always* cross paths. Each ghost or spirit you encounter can offer a lesson in history.

Before or after your ghost hunt, take the time to do the research. It's well worth the time. If you're in a group, have one or two people assigned to delve into the research and then fill in the rest of the members. It's an exciting aspect to ghost hunting. Most ghost stories are based on true history, even if just loosely. Knowing the truth about the events leading up to a haunting can help you better understand and discover the differences between what is actually paranormal and what are merely urban legends.

I had such a wonderful time visiting some of the locations from this book. Please take the time and explore some of the old mansions and museums in Akron for yourself. As for the other locations, please be careful. Never go alone and always get permission. I cannot stress that enough. Trespassing is against the law; getting caught as a ghost hunter or paranormal investigator makes it that much harder for serious researchers like myself. So please act professionally, obey the law and, again, get permission. Please be responsible if you go out hunting for ghosts.

Visit the Haunted Akron website at www.hauntedakron.info for information on local ghost hunts and explorations. We also gladly accept any additional stories relating to this book or your own experiences and paranormal evidence.

All historical events in this book have been researched and written according to the information gathered from various newspapers, firsthand witnesses and the written accounts of local historians. Other stories and locations were investigated and visited by myself. I went to extreme lengths to make sure that everything is as accurate as possible.

Appendix I
COMMON PARANORMAL TERMS

agent: A human being, typically a teenage female, who unknowingly directs poltergeist energy.

amulet: An object that has the power to ward off ghosts and evil spirits.

angel: Benevolent spiritual beings that help and watch over people.

apparition: The disembodied soul or spirit that can be seen visually.

atmospheric apparition: Not actually a ghost or spirit, but instead a "visual imprint" of people and events that was left behind in the environment and continues to replay.

aura: A field of energy believed by some to surround living creatures.

automatic writing: A type of communication with ghosts or spirits by which they take control over the writer's hand and write out a message.

automatism: An unconscious or spontaneous muscular movement caused by ghosts or spirits. Automatic writing is one form of automatism.

banshee (or *bean-sidhe*): Ominous warning spirits of Scotland and Ireland.

channeling: A form of spirit communication by which an unseen entity possesses a medium in a controlled environment to impart guidance and wisdom or predict future events. The entity could be a deceased human being or other spirit.

clairvoyance: Either an internal or external vision of present or future events, objects, places and people.

cold reading: A psychic reading given with no prior knowledge of the sitter.

collective apparition: A ghost or spirit sighting seen simultaneously by more than one living person.

crisis apparition: Ghosts that appear to loved ones and close friends just before or soon after their deaths.

crossroads: Point where two roads intersect—said to be a focal point of supernatural energy.

deathbed apparitions: See crisis apparition.

demon: Fallen angels associated with evil.

direct voice phenomenon (DVP): The voice of a ghost or spirit being spoken to the sitters of a séance. The voice usually comes from some point near the medium but not through the medium. Sometimes a spirit horn or trumpet is used.

direct writing: When a ghost or spirit's handwriting appears directly on a previously unmarked, unwritten surface.

dowsing: The paranormal detection of underground water or mineral deposits (or lost persons and objects) using a divining rod or pendulum.

earth lights: See ghost lights.

ectoplasm: A solid, liquid or vaporous substance said to be produced by ghosts or spirits; it is usually a milky white color and has an ozone smell.

electromagnetic field (EMF) detectors: Hand-held scientific instruments that can pick up electronic and magnetic fields over different frequencies. They can read changes and distortions in the normal electromagnetic fields.

electronic voice phenomenon (EVP): The attempt to capture a ghost or spirit's voice on audio recording tapes. Typically there is no voice heard for the people present in the recording, but after reviewing the tapes, there are strange voices recorded.

elemental spirit: A spirit associated with one of the classical four elements (fire, earth, air and water).

exorcism: A religious rite used to cast out a ghost, spirit or entity from a living person's body or a particular location.

extrasensory perception (ESP): The acquisition of information by means beyond the five human senses.

fairy: A small, humanlike, mythical being—may be benevolent or malevolent.

false awakening: An experience in which a person believes that he or she has woken up but actually is still dreaming.

focal person: A person who is at the center of poltergeist activity.

ghost: The visual appearance of a spirit or soul of a deceased being, human or animal—the disembodied soul or life force.

ghostbuster: A living person who can remove an unwanted ghost, spirit, entity or poltergeist activity from a particular location.

ghost catcher: A wind chime that makes noise as a ghost or spirit passes by.

ghost hunt: An attempt made by the living to find and see a ghost or spirit.

ghost hunter: A living individual who searches out and sometimes finds and identifies ghosts and spirits.

ghost investigation: A scientific endeavor, in a controlled environment, set up to communicate, record and capture visual evidence of the existence of ghosts.

ghost lights: Luminous phenomena typically shaped in ball form or irregular patches of light appearing randomly and defying explanation.

ghoul: An evil spirit or monster that robs graves and feeds off the flesh of the dead.

gray lady: The ghost of a woman who has died at the hands of a lover or waits for the return of a loved one.

guardian angel: An angel believed to protect the individual.

hallucination: A false and distorted perception of reality.

haunt: A place where a ghost or ghosts frequently return.

haunted objects: Jewelry, furniture, clothing and such that appear to be haunted by a past owner or have been cursed.

haunting: The continuous manifestation of inexplicable phenomena associated with the presence of ghosts or spirits attached to a particular location.

levitation: The paranormal raising or suspension of an object or person.

ley lines: Invisible lines that run between sacred objects or locations.

luminous phenomena: The experience of strange lights or glows, often around objects or people.

Marian apparition: The appearance of the Virgin Mary.

materialization: The manifestation of physical objects, animals or people.

medium: A person with a gift to communicate with ghosts and spirits on behalf of the living.

modern apparitions: "New" ghosts of deceased individuals. They appear in fashion from the current time.

near-death experience (NDE): A phenomenon in which a person clinically dies or comes very close to death, only to be revived; the person can often recall in great detail stories of spiritual worlds and other supernatural events.

necromancer: A person usually considered a wizard or sorcerer and who can raise the dead and command the spirits to obtain information about the future.

orb: A mass of energy in the shape of a ball. There are several classifications depending on size. Ghostly apparitions are usually always associated with an orb.

Ouija board: A board with letters and numbers used by people who are attempting to communicate with ghosts or spirits.

out-of-body experience (OBE): Also called astral projection, it is the phenomenon in which a living person's spirit can exit the body, travel the earth and other spiritual worlds and then return back to the body.

paranormal: Something that is beyond the normal.

parapsychology: The scientific study of unusual events associated with the human experience and psi subjects.

percipient: A living person who sees a ghost, spirit or paranormal event.

phantom animals: Ghosts of deceased animals.

phantom hitchhiker: A ghost or spirit that haunts a particular stretch of road or route. Phantom hitchhikers ask for rides only to suddenly disappear when they reach their destination.

photographic apparitions: Ghosts and spirits that you can't see but instead appear in photographs after they are developed.

planchette: A pointer used with a Ouija board to communicate with ghosts, spirits or higher-plane entities.

poltergeist: "Noisy ghost." Poltergeists are invisible masses of spirit energy that may or may not be connected to a living human agent. Some of the most common poltergeist activities include loud and unexplained noise, levitations, the moving of objects and electrical problems.

possession: When a person's mind and body are taken over by ghosts, spirits or other supernatural entities such as demons.

precognition: The paranormal awareness of future events.

psi: A general term used to denote the unknown factors responsible for a variety of paranormal phenomena.

psychic: Popular term used to denote a person who regularly uses, or who appears to be especially gifted with, psi abilities.

psychic echo: When sounds from the past have mysteriously recorded themselves into the natural environment.

psychokinesis (PK): Mind movement; the apparent ability to influence the environment by intention alone.

radio voice phenomenon (RVP): The voice of a ghost or spirit communicating through a regular radio.

reciprocal apparition: An experience in which both the agent and the ghost or spirit see and react to each other.

recurring apparitions: Ghosts or spirits that appear in regular cycles, usually once a year—on the anniversary of their deaths, for example.

repressed psychokinetic energy: A theoretical psychic force unconsciously produced by an individual while undergoing a physical or mental trauma.

retrocognition: Paranormal knowledge of past events.

scrying: A type of prophecy in which an individual can see future events by staring into a shiny or reflective surface, such as a mirror or crystal ball.

séance: The gathering of a group of individuals for the purpose of communicating with the ghosts of the dead.

sensitive: Someone who is aware or can detect paranormal events beyond the range of the five human senses.

screaming skulls: Human skulls that protest with poltergeist activity when their final wishes are not fulfilled.

shaman: A witch doctor or medicine man who communicates with spirits while in a trance and who has the power of healing.

sixth sense: Popular term for ESP.

sleep paralysis: A frightening state of seeming to be awake but being unable to move.

soul: The spiritual life force or essence carrying an individual's personality and consciousness of all actions.

specter: A ghost or apparition.

spirit: Often used to define the soul of a person, a spirit can also be used to represent places such as sacred lakes or objects, shrines and elemental entities.

spirit detection: The reading made by scientific equipment (EMF detectors, temperature changes and so on) when a ghost or spirit is present.

spirit photography: Photographs of figures or faces, believed by some to be those of deceased persons.

spirit profile: Researching the background and history of the ghost or spirit and determining its consistent patterns as a result of the findings.

spiritualism: Belief that ghosts and spirits can and do communicate with the living.

spook lights: See ghost lights.

supernatural: Something that exists or occurs through some means other than any known force in nature or science.

telepathy: Mind-to-mind communication.

telephone calls from the dead: When a person receives a telephone call from someone who is dead. The person may or may not know that the caller is deceased.

transportation apparitions: The appearance of ghostly cars, trucks, ships, bicycles, carriages, trains, airplanes and anything else that carries people. They frequently haunt their old routes.

vortex: An opening or doorway between our world and the spirit world.

wild hunt: A group of ghost horsemen or packs of ghostly dogs seen at night.

witch: A woman with supernatural powers.

wraith: A ghost that comes back to avenge its own death; considered an omen spirit.

Appendix II
LOCAL PARANORMAL GROUPS

CLEVELAND SUPERNATURAL INVESTIGATIONS—Cleveland Supernatural Investigations, or CSI for short, is a group of like-minded individuals, based out of the Cleveland area, dedicated to investigating and researching unexplained paranormal phenomena in the Ohio or Great Lakes region. www.clevelandsupernatural.com.

CUYAHOGA VALLEY PARANORMAL—A paranormal investigative team doing serious investigations in Ohio and surrounding areas. We use the most current investigation techniques combined with historical research to obtain evidence of life after death and to preserve history. Author Jeri Holland is director. www.hauntedcuyahoga.net.

LAKE ERIE PARANORMAL—Lake Erie Paranormal is a nonprofit paranormal investigation and research team based out of Toledo, Ohio. However, the organization also does investigations throughout all of Ohio and southeast Michigan. www.lakeerieparanormal.net.

MOONSPENDERS—Author and paranormal investigator Ken Summers offers a website containing local stories, gay/lesbian hauntings, and various railroad ghost stories. www.moonspenders.com

MUNROE FALLS PARANORMAL SOCIETY—The Munroe Falls Paranormal Society strives to provide an objective and unbiased approach to the scientific study, investigation and research of paranormal phenomena. www.munroe-falls-paranormal-society.com.

OHIO GHOST HUNTERS SOCIETY—OGHS does real scientific research, employing topical scientific theory to practical application. You won't find made-up "fairy tale" theories, speculation, conjecture or assumption here. If they can't prove it and show you the proof, you won't see it on the organization's website. www.ohioghs.net.

OHIO PARANORMAL INVESTIGATION NETWORK—The Ohio Paranormal Investigation Network (OPIN) is a database of personal investigations in conjunction with various reports and documentations on ghosts or other paranormal activity. This website is for informational service only and is based strictly on opinion. OPIN is looking to help those who are encountering situations they feel are attributed to ghosts or other possible paranormal activity. www.ghosthelp.net.

WESTERN RESERVE PARANORMAL—A northeast Ohio paranormal group that seeks to help others with problems of a ghostly nature, whether that is removing the spirits or teaching how to live with their "spirited" roommates. www.westernreserveparanormal.com.

WORLD PARANORMAL INVESTIGATIONS—WPI is based out of northeast Ohio and the West Midlands. This group was started so that two countries could come together and share paranormal experiences, as well as investigate paranormal activity. www.wpiusauk.com.

SOURCES

Akron (OH) Daily Beacon, 1869–90.

Akron (OH) Daily Democrat, 1892–1902.

Ancestry.com. Genealogy, Family Trees and Family History Records Online. www.ancestry.com.

Bierce, Lucious V. *Historical Reminiscences of Summit County*. Akron, OH: T&HG Canfield, 1854.

Bloetscher, Virginia Chase. *Indians of the Cuyahoga Valley and Vicinity*. Akron, OH: North American Indian Cultural Center, 1980.

Canal Plat Maps, 1892–1904, 1912. Ohio Historical Society, Columbus, Ohio, 1989.

Doyle, William B. *Centennial History of Summit County, Ohio and Representative Citizens*. Chicago, IL: Biographical Publishing, 1908.

Fielder, David G. *Turkeyfoot Island History, Portage Lakes Area, Summit County, Ohio....* Akron, OH: D.G. Fielder, 2000.

Gieck, Jack. *Early Akron's Industrial Valley: A History of the Cascade Locks*. Kent, OH: Kent State University Press, 2008.

Google Maps. www.maps.google.com.

Grismer, Karl H. *Akron and Summit County*. Akron, OH: Summit County Historical Society, 1952.

Hern, Herbert F. *The Portage Trail: A Historic Indian Portage from Lake Erie to Lake Chautauqua*. Mayville, NY: Chautauqua County Council of Boy Scouts of America, 1971.

Holland, Jeri. "Cuyahoga Falls History," January 4, 1997. www.cuyahogafallshistory.com.

———. "History of Akron and Summit County," October 2001. www.akronhistory.org.

Jesensky, Joseph D. *An Archaeological Survey of the Cuyahoga River Valley: From the Cuyahoga Gorge—Summit County to Independence—Cuyahoga County, Ohio.* Cuyahoga Falls, OH: Northampton Historical Society, 1979.

Jesensky, Joseph D., and Chuck Ayers. *Joe's Place: Conversations on the Cuyahoga Valley.* Peninsula, OH: Cuyahoga Valley Association, 1999.

Lane, Samuel A. *Fifty Years and Over of Akron and Summit County.* Akron, OH: Beacon Job Department, 1892.

Nye, Pearl R., and Cloea Thomas. *Scenes and Songs of the Ohio-Erie Canal: Photographs and Songs.* Columbus: Ohio Historical Society, 1971.

Olin, Oscar Eugene, and James A. Braden. *A Centennial History of Akron, 1825–1925.* Akron, OH: Summit County Historical Society, 1925.

Perrin, William Henry, and A.A. Graham. *History of Summit County.* Chicago, IL: Baskin and Battery, 1881.

Peterson, Richard M. *Marking the Trail of the Portage Path: Pinpointing the Exact Location of the Trail—Survey Data.* Akron, OH: Yeck Family Portage Path Memorial Program, 2002.

Seguin, Marilyn. *Silver Ribbon Skinny: The Towpath Adventures of Skinny Nye, a Muleskinner on the Ohio and Erie Canal, 1884.* Boston, MA: Branden Publishing, 1996.

Summit County (Akron, OH) Beacon, 1857–1910.

Summit County Chapter of the Ohio Genealogical Society. *Glendale Cemetery Burial Records: Formerly Akron Rural Cemetery.* Akron, OH: Summit County Chapter, Ohio Genealogical Society, 2000.

ABOUT THE AUTHOR

F rom family photos to important historical events about her hometown of Cuyahoga Falls, Ohio, Jeri Holland has dedicated passion, time, knowledge and colossal effort in the pursuit of compiling and documenting the treasured past. She has created websites Cuyahoga Falls History (www.cuyahogafallshistory.com) and History of Akron & Summit County (www.akronhistory.org) and joined several historical societies, including the Cuyahoga Falls Historical Society and the Summit County Historical Society, to share this past with anyone who wishes to know it.

From this love of history comes a love of paranormal history. Jeri has spent many hours studying firsthand what goes bump in the night, be it in the dark woods or run-down sanitariums and prisons. She believes that without historical context, the stories and legends of the haunted present wouldn't be nearly as fascinating or spooky. Jeri is the creator and director of the paranormal group Cuyahoga Valley Paranormal and designed and operates the websites www.hauntedcuyahoga.net and www.hauntedakron. info. She uses this perspective when speaking about the paranormal world on the radio and television and in print, like with WNIR, 19 Action News and *Cleveland Scene* magazine. For those who share her passion for historical hauntings, she currently provides a variety of classes about the paranormal at the Quirk Cultural Center in Cuyahoga Falls throughout the year and delivers information through lectures at public libraries. Jeri also shares her experience of investigating eerie places by organizing community events such as haunted scavenger hunts and hikes. Imparting the fact that the world is far more mysterious than what we see and hear every day is Jeri's goal; the goose bumps aren't bad either.

Visit us at
www.historypress.net